20 Surprisingly Simple Rules and Tools
for a Great Marriage

TYNDALE HOUSE PUBLISHERS, INC., Wheaton, Illinois

Surprisingly Simple

20 RULES
and TOOLS
for a GREAT
MARRIAGE

DR. STEVE STEPHENS

Visit Tyndale's exciting Web site at www.tyndale.com

Edited by Lisa A. Jackson

Designed by Zandrah Maguigad

Library of Congress Cataloging-in-Publication Data

Stephens, Steve.
  20 surprisingly simple rules and tools for a great marriage / Steve Stephens.
    p. cm.
ISBN 0-8423-6203-7 (sc)
1. Marriage—Religious aspects—Christianity. 2. Spouses—Religious life. I. Title: Twenty surprisingly simple rules and tools for a great marriage. II. Title.

BV4596.M3 S737 2002
248.8′44—dc21   2002010949

Printed in the United States of America

09 08 07 06 05 04
10 9   8   7   6

CONTENTS

Getting Started vii

RULE ❶: Make Your Spouse a Priority 1

RULE ❷: Accept Differences 5

RULE ❸: Listen Carefully 11

RULE ❹: Compliment Daily 17

RULE ❺: Work Together As a Team 23

RULE ❻: Mind Your Manners 31

RULE ❼: Watch Less TV 37

RULE ❽: Find Time for Fun 43

RULE ❾: Do the Little Things 49

RULE ❿: Celebrate the "Top Five" 55

RULE ⓫: Think Positive 61

RULE ⓬: Fight Fair 67

RULE ⓭: Forgive 73

RULE ⓮: Welcome Each Other Home 81

RULE ⓯: Go to Bed at the Same Time 87

RULE ⓰: Develop Mutual Friends 93

RULE ⓱: Take a Date 101

RULE ⓲: Make Love 109

RULE ⓳: Pray for Your Spouse 117

RULE ⓴: Treasure Your Spouse 125

Wrapping Up 133

GETTING STARTED

"Don't burp!"

Dusty, my eight-year-old son, and I were driving to the radio station where I host a live talk show. He was my guest on this particular day and he was telling me what he thought the rules of radio might be.

He thought for a moment and then gave me his list:

1. Don't burp.
2. Don't fluff.
3. Don't spill your water.
4. Don't fall off your chair.
5. Don't bang your head on the microphone.

"Those are excellent rules," I said.

After the show Dusty was more quiet than usual. "What's wrong?" I asked.

"I didn't do very well on the radio, did I?" he said.

"Dusty, you did great!"

"Dad, you're just saying that."

"No, I mean it," I reassured him.

"But Dad," he said with a downcast look, "I broke four of the five rules."

Life is full of rules. There are work rules, traffic rules, social rules—rules for almost everything. Recently, I attended a soccer game of my other son,

Dylan. As I was watching, a boy bent down to tie his shoe. The coach yelled out, "Don't tie your shoe when the ball is in play."

One more rule.

While we may not like some of them—like the stipulation that we can't go fifty miles per hour down a residential street even if we're in a hurry—we know most rules aren't there just to frustrate us. They're in place to protect us and to help our society run smoothly.

Even marriage has its rules, and they are surprisingly simple. Most of them are obvious, but they are also incredibly powerful. If you follow them, your marriage will improve. In fact, some couples have told me that these rules have saved their marriage. But if you ignore the rules, your marriage will suffer.

So don't fight it. Learn the rules. Memorize them. Act on them.

You'll be shocked at how these twenty surprisingly simple rules can make a good marriage even better and can save a struggling marriage from falling apart.

All it takes is two people who are both willing to work together. If you both give it an honest try . . .

> you will grow closer
> you will be healthier
> you will be happier
> you will be so glad you discovered the rules

As you turn the pages of this book, you'll find twenty practical rules that I have discovered in my work with hundreds of couples over the past twenty-five years as a psychologist specializing in marriage and family issues. These rules also came from personal life experience. I've been married to my wife, Tami, for eighteen years, and we've known each other much longer. I've learned the importance of these rules by finding out what happens when you break them. I'm still learning (just ask Tami), but I'm better now than I was a year or two ago. And hopefully, I'll be even better a year or two from now.

Rules from professional and personal experience are important, but they aren't the most crucial thing. Everything I discover as a psychologist and marriage counselor, I run through the grid of the Holy Bible. God's Word is my foundation, and with it as my frame of reference, I know I will not stray far from the truth. And the truth is what ultimately matters!

Each chapter in this book will explain one of the rules and show why it's important. After each rule, you'll find three tools. I've included these tools because while information might make interesting reading, it's the application of that information that makes a great marriage. These three tools will help you to apply the rules in a way that is simple but profound. The tools are:

Prayer: A way to seek God's help in getting you on track
and keeping you there
Passage: A quotation from the Holy Bible that will give you
God's perspective
Practice: A few assignments to help you insert the rules into
the ups and downs of everyday life

By now you're probably ready to jump into the rules. So read on and watch as your marriage:

grows strong
grows deep
grows better
grows positive
grows more and more beautiful

RULE ❶
MAKE YOUR SPOUSE A PRIORITY

"IF ONLY I WAS IMPORTANT to my husband," said Susan.

"But he says he loves you."

"Maybe he loves me," she said, "but it sure seems like his job and his friends and his boat and his football games are all a lot more important to him than I am. I feel like I'm at the very bottom of his list."

I hear this sort of complaint over and over when I counsel couples. Most of us take better care of our cars and houses than we do our marriages. Too often, we take one another for granted. We treat our marriages like those annoying pink mechanical bunnies; we pop in a battery and then forget about them, assuming they'll go on forever. But the reality is that if we don't take care of our relationships, they will eventually stop working.

In order to thrive, your marriage must be your number one priority—at the top of your list. And your spouse needs to see this every day. The principle is simple: If your partner doesn't feel she is special to you, sooner or later she'll be tempted to find someone who does make her feel special.

It's not easy to keep marriage at the top of your priority list when there are so many other demands on your time: demanding jobs, demanding children, and other demanding responsibilities. While each has its place in your life, developing a healthy marriage is most important and should be given more attention than your other responsibilities.

When my friend Ralph realized that his long workweeks were causing problems in his marriage, he promised his wife he would spend more time with her. The next day he nervously went to his boss's office to declare that he could no longer work as much overtime because it was not healthy for his marriage.

His boss listened without saying a word. When Ralph finished, his boss smiled, patted Ralph on the back, and said, "You're just the sort of person I respect. You know how to keep your priorities in perspective and you have the guts to take a stand." The next day, Ralph received a significant promotion, a raise in pay, and the promise of no more overtime.

While taking a stand might not give results as positive for you as it did for Ralph, it's sure to improve your marriage.

A healthy marriage benefits others as well. It's the best gift you can give your children, whether those children are three years old or sixty-three. Knowing that their parents are together creates a real feeling of security and stability for children.

On the flip side, balancing the parent role and the marriage role can be difficult. One of the worst mistakes a parent can make is to allow children to take priority over a spouse. While you might think you're simply helping your children, it doesn't work that way. Focusing primarily on the children can threaten your marriage's stability, and when your marriage loses stability, your children will suffer.

When classic-movie star Lauren Bacall discovered she was pregnant, she excitedly broke the news to her husband, actor Humphrey Bogart. He turned away and began to cry.

"What's wrong?" she asked. "Aren't you happy?"

"I'm happy, but I'm also very sad," was his reply.

"Why?"

"Because once you have a child, I'll never be as important to you as I am now."

It's natural for parents to love their children, but when a spouse places children at the top of his priority list, the other partner often begins to feel resentful toward both the children and the spouse. Don't allow this to happen in your marriage. Make your marriage strong by letting your spouse know that her needs come first, even before the children's.

Stop right now and make a mental list of all the ways you can let your spouse know he's your number one priority. Be creative. Then start today to implement your ideas.

What's so exciting about doing this is that as you begin to make your spouse a priority, you'll be showing your love to her—and she'll start communicating that love back to you. The old saying is true: The more you give, the more you get. And as the love between the two of you begins to flow stronger, you will begin to feel a spark of joy and passion that can reenergize your marriage, making it what you always hoped it would be. And maybe more.

TODAY'S TOOLS

Prayer

Dear God,

Help me to keep life in the proper perspective. Help me to love the one you gave me with all my heart, even when I don't feel like it. When I get distracted by all that must be done, remind me to take the time and effort to communicate that my partner is my first priority.

Forgive me for all the times I have ignored my spouse—all those times I have let people or things or activities take up time that should have been spent with him.

Forgive me for all those times I gave my partner only what was left after everybody and everything else had had its share.

Teach me to be more generous and less greedy, more sensitive and less selfish, more focused and less hectic.

Teach me how to show love to my spouse every single day.

Amen

Passage

So again I say, each man must love his wife as he loves himself, and the wife must respect her husband. EPHESIANS 5:33

Practice

① Tell your spouse that she is at the top of your list and promise her that you won't let anything push her from that rightful position.
② Next time your spouse asks you to do something, do it with no excuse, procrastination, or complaint.
③ Ask your spouse how you can pray for him during the day, and then commit to doing it.
④ Set the alarm fifteen minutes early so you can cuddle up together and talk about the day ahead before you have to get up.

RULE ❷
ACCEPT DIFFERENCES

MARY LOVES SPENDING TIME with other people. If there's a party, she wants to be there. But Jim, Mary's husband, is an introvert and a homebody. Jim would rather spend a quiet evening with a good book than attend a party. When Mary and Jim were first married, the differences in their personalities caused major conflict. Although Mary accepted every social invitation that came along, Jim usually dug in his heels and refused to leave the house.

Tensions built and tempers flared.

Mary and Jim had to learn to accept and work with their differences. Now they go out as a couple two nights a week and Mary can be as social as she wishes. Three nights a week they stay at home and Jim enjoys the peace of a quiet house. On the other two nights, Mary sometimes makes an effort to get together with friends on her own because she knows that Jim enjoys spending time alone.

Every couple has its differences. Maybe a spender has married a saver. Or a highly structured person is drawn to someone who celebrates spontaneity. Or a collector who likes a certain amount of clutter has married a tosser who draws great joy from clearing away the clutter.

God clearly has a sense of humor. He made us so that opposites attract. Often, once we get together, we drive each other crazy. As I counsel couples, I find that invariably it's these differences that cause the most difficulty in a marriage.

Sometimes it's easy to let differences get the best of you, and you begin to believe that you're just too incompatible to make your marriage work.

Nonsense!

We are all incompatible in some area or another. If compatibility were the main criteria for a great marriage, everyone would give up. Sure, some couples are more compatible than others, but that doesn't necessarily make their marriages better.

If you and your spouse share a common faith with a true commitment to that faith, you already have a core value system that can help you deal with all the other differences you face.

If the two of you were completely alike, your relationship would be boring and out of balance. I know a couple who are both spenders. They have a lot of fun, but they also have seventeen credit cards filled to the max. I knew another couple who were both savers. In forty-two years of marriage they never took a single vacation and they rarely went out to a restaurant. They accumulated great wealth, but they never enjoyed it. Now they've both passed away and their children are enjoying a terrific inheritance.

God knows that balance is important; that's why he gave you a spouse who is so different from you. Thank him for those differences. Don't try to pressure your partner into thinking or feeling or acting like you do. Instead, make an effort to understand and appreciate the differences.

If you grumble or nag, you will become bitter. If you fight, you will become frustrated. But if you relax and accept the differences as a blessing, you will learn the art of flexibility and compromise. You will grow in maturity, and the texture of your life will become richer. In the end, you will develop into a better person—a person of character and compassion.

Remember Mary and Jim? Mary taught Jim to enjoy the company of crowds, and Jim taught Mary the value of a peaceful night at home. They both still have their preferences, but they've learned to appreciate something different. Mary saved Jim from isolation, and Jim saved Mary from social burnout. Together they have become deeper, more balanced, and closer to one another.

Most conflicts are not about major moral or ethical issues but about different preferences. She wants it her way and he wants it his. The Bible asks, "What causes fights and quarrels among you?" In the next verse it answers its own question: "You want something but don't get it" (James 4:1-2, NIV).

As we learn to accept that we won't always have to have it our way, marriage becomes a lot easier. After a while we realize that most of our fights are either stupid or selfish. In fact, if someone had secretly videotaped our last few fights with our spouses, most of us would be quite embarrassed.

As you learn to respect each other's differences, you'll find that you aren't fighting as much and that you're actually moving closer to each other.

Tami and I have very different tastes in music. What she likes, I usually don't, and vice versa. So she has her CDs and I have mine. Hers are kept in one room and mine in another. For a long time, this seemed like a great compromise.

But over the years something amazing has happened. I have come to like some of her CDs, and she has begun to like some of mine. No, it's not a miracle; it's the marvel of marriage. As we have grown closer over time, our differences have begun to blend. It started with just one CD, but now there are nearly twenty that we both like. We keep these CDs in a special place, and whenever I put one in the player, we both smile, knowing that no matter how strong our differences, there's always hope.

As you begin to accept the ways in which you and your spouse are different, you will begin to grow closer together. And as you grow closer, the differences will no longer seem like such a big deal.

TODAY'S TOOLS

Prayer

Dear God,

Thank you for making my partner just the way she is—with all her strengths and weaknesses and differences.

Before the earth was formed you dreamed of my spouse. When the time was right you shaped her soul and watched her life grow into what it is today. It is no accident that the two of us are together. Yet there are days when our togetherness is challenged by our differences.

Help me to accept what you have given me. Help me to rejoice in our differences, rather than merely tolerating them.

Forgive me for the many times I have been less than respectful—those times I have not paid proper attention or have not acted upon my spouse's words and ways which were different from my own.

Amen

Passage

So accept each other just as Christ has accepted you; then God will be glorified. ROMANS 15:7

Practice

① Take your spouse to dinner and make a list of as many differences as you can think of. Thank your partner for those differences.

② The next time you have an argument with your spouse, ask yourself, "Is this really about preferences?" Then try to see the issue from your spouse's perspective. You might even try doing things his way.

③ Don't force her to do it your way. Catch yourself before saying something negative, critical, or arrogant about how your partner did something. Bite your tongue and smile.

RULE ❸
LISTEN CAREFULLY

"WHEN YOU'RE OUT and about today, would you stop by the grocery store and pick up milk, baking soda, oatmeal, and a few apples?" Julie asked.

"No problem," said Mike, heading out the door. Twenty minutes later, Mike stood in the local grocery store, trying to remember what Julie had asked him to buy.

"Why don't you ever listen to me?" Julie asked when Mike handed her the bag filled with milk, bread, ice cream, and potatoes.

"At least I remembered the milk," said Mike.

"And your ice cream," said Julie, walking out the door and slamming it behind her.

Mike had heard, but he hadn't really listened. We all do it. It seems simple enough, but at times all of us have trouble really listening. Listening means stopping what you're doing, looking at your spouse, and truly hearing each word.

The number one complaint from wives who divorce their husbands is that their husbands don't listen to them or take them seriously. So guys, put down your newspapers and turn off your television sets. If you don't learn to listen, you might be the next statistic.

Part of the problem with listening is that men and women are wired differently. Most men like to get right to the point, and if the point isn't made in the first three sentences, their minds tend to wander. So wives can help us guys a lot by doing what most newspaper articles do: summarize the major points of the story in the first paragraph. Tell us who, what, where, and when in the first few sentences. Then follow with the little details.

When you're talking to your husband, start with three sentences and then stop. Follow up with a question like, "What do you think of that?" "Why is this happening?" or "What should I do next?"

Wait patiently for a response and then listen without interruption until he's finished talking. Then offer three more sentences and a few more questions. When he's not feeling overwhelmed by too much information, a man will usually be more responsive.

It's important for men to realize that our wives yearn to connect with us. To connect often means to talk. If we don't listen and talk to our wives, they'll think we don't care about what they're saying. If this continues, they might even begin to believe that since we don't care about what they're saying, we don't care about them.

If you don't listen, your partner might stop talking. She might grow silent and withdrawn, disconnecting from you completely.

Really listening is an intimate activity. The more you listen, the more your partner will open his heart to you. As you spend time talking and listening to one another, the two of you will grow closer and begin to build a healthy, thriving relationship. It is through talking and listening that the two of you can become emotionally one. Remember when you were dating? You would sit for hours, talking and listening and basking in the glow of each other. You were quick to hear and slow to speak. You wanted to learn more about each other, so you clung to every word and were excited by all that you heard. You can return to that time. All you need to do is listen.

You must listen for more than just words. Listen to the tone of voice. Listen for the mood. Listen to her needs and fears and hopes and hurts. Start by getting rid of your preconceived notions. Listen as if you have just met. You are not the same person as when the two of you first met, and neither is your spouse. There is so much more to learn. Listen with young, fresh ears. You might be surprised by what you will hear.

Thousands of couples come to my office for help, some married a year or two and others who have just celebrated their fiftieth wedding anniversary. I often spend time listening to the husband and wife separately from one another. I listen carefully, asking questions to dig deeper and clarify what I'm hearing. When I bring the two together to talk about what I've heard, it's not unusual for the husband or wife to lean forward and ask, "How did you know that about my partner?"

"I listen very closely," is my usual reply.

William Shakespeare writes of "the disease of not listening." This is an excellent metaphor, for a disease can be deadly either physically, emotionally, or maritally. If an oncologist said I had cancer, he would have my attention. If he said, "Do such and such, or you will not survive," you can bet that I would do whatever he said.

Not listening is a relationship disease. It can kill your love and marriage. Millions of relationships have already died from this disease, and what is so sad is that it is completely curable. Many of us have this disease and we don't even know it. The disease can eat away at your marriage while you move through your life naïvely unaware that danger is just around the corner. There is good news, though. The cure is as simple as three little words:

Stop
Look
Listen

Using this simple solution you can block the disease of not listening, strengthen your relationship, and save your marriage.

Start today and listen carefully to your spouse. You will be amazed at how quickly this simple rule will bring a sparkle to his eye.

TODAY'S TOOLS

Prayer

Dear God,

Help me to listen—really listen.

Help me to listen to you, God.

Help me to listen to what is true and noble and right.

Help me to listen carefully and caringly to the special partner you have given me.

Forgive me for how often I have neglected the words and heart and hurts of my beloved.

Forgive me for being more focused on explaining or defending or disputing than on really listening. Remind me daily that showing I care is more important than proving I am right.

Show me how to listen with my whole heart and full attention.

Amen

Passage

My dear brothers and sisters, be quick to listen, slow to speak, and slow to get angry. JAMES 1:19

Practice

① The next time your spouse talks to you, put down whatever you are doing and look her in the eye. Make an effort to truly listen.

② When your spouse talks to you, practice repeating back to him what you just heard.

③ Try to use the three-sentences-with-a-question method when talking to your spouse sometime in the next twenty-four hours.

RULE ❹
COMPLIMENT DAILY

EVERYBODY LOVES A COMPLIMENT.

Mark Twain once said that he could live a full month on nothing but a single compliment.

The next time you meet someone at work or at church or even at the local grocery store, compliment that person and watch the reaction. Chances are he will smile. Chances are you just made his day.

While we all enjoy receiving a compliment, most of us aren't very good at giving them. Some people think complimentary things but rarely share them for fear of sounding silly. Others aren't even sure how to give a compliment. Perhaps they were never complimented as children, and now they subconsciously carry on the pattern of silence. Still others are simply too lazy. A good compliment takes work, and some people don't have the time, energy, or inclination to make the effort.

If you're looking for ways to improve your marriage, you can start with a compliment.

There are many different types of compliments. While each type is appreciated, some will be more treasured than others.

One type is a compliment of **possession.** One might say, "What an incredible car," or "I love your earrings." These compliments, though a bit superficial, provide a good place to start if you aren't used to complimenting your spouse.

Second, there are compliments of **appearance.**

"You look wonderful," or "That shirt really shows off your eyes." These compliments are more personal and let your spouse know that you find him desirable. We all like to be complimented on our appearance, but it's common to receive this kind of affirmation more from friends and relatives than from our partner. This is sad, because we most want and even need this appreciation from our spouse.

If your spouse doesn't compliment your appearance, don't look for it elsewhere. Talk to your partner about how you wish to please him. Find out what you could do to encourage more of these compliments, and then try some of these things. On the other hand, if you haven't complimented your spouse lately, it's time to start. Don't miss a powerful opportunity to communicate your love and strengthen your relationship.

A third type of compliment is related to **behavior.**

When your spouse does something good or kind or sacrificial, what do you say? Too often a spouse says nothing. I recently heard a psychologist explain that it's normal for a couple to take each other for granted. He said we should accept this as the typical progression of marriage—the longer we are married, the more you take each other for granted.

Well, I refuse to accept this. It's not right, nor is it healthy.

Your spouse does a lot that deserves your appreciation. Maybe it's keeping the house or yard in order; it might be managing children or finances; it could even be going to work or to the grocery store. Most people like to be recognized for a job well done. My wife, Tami, works hard to keep up with all the everyday tasks that need to be done for a family of five, and she appreciates it when I thank her. Unfortunately, sometimes I get so busy and distracted that I fail to notice all that she's doing. When I neglect to compliment her for her hard work, it's easy for her to become discouraged.

Our friend Susan had no idea how much Randy did around the house until a car accident forced him to remain in the hospital for a month. Now that he's recovered, Susan thanks him often for the hundreds of things he does that she once took for granted. In addition, the compliments and encouragements Randy received from Susan reminded him that he also needed to acknowledge his wife's acts of service. So now they both look for opportunities to compliment each other's behavior.

"You are such a wonderful cook," Randy says.

"And you go to work each day without complaint," says Susan. "Thank you."

When you feel appreciated, you tend to feel loved.

The fourth type of compliment is the most powerful of all. This is the compliment of **character.**

Tami is one of the most generous people I know. She gives to her friends and family and neighbors. If anyone needs anything, Tami does whatever she can to meet the need. She watches the neighbor kids, volunteers at the local grade school, works in the church nursery, takes meals to the sick, and performs hundreds of other acts of kindness. There are times I think she is too generous for her own good.

Yet it's important that I compliment Tami for this noble trait. Every time I see her selflessly reach out to others, I try to let her know how much I appreciate her.

Compliments of character—such as kindness, courage, responsibility, or wisdom—may be best, but any compliment is good. Make a list of sincere and personal compliments for your spouse, then every day offer at least one.

It will make a difference, I assure you. You will encourage your spouse.

You'll make him smile. You'll draw him closer to you and you will improve your marriage.

TODAY'S TOOLS

Prayer

Dear God,

I have so much to be thankful for, and yet so often I am better at complaining than showing my appreciation.

Give me a grateful heart.

Open my eyes to the many things my spouse brings to my life—to enrich, teach, comfort, and make me a better person.

Open my mouth to share lovingly and humbly all the things I should speak much more often than I have.

Forgive me for all the opportunities I've had to compliment that I haven't even noticed.

Forgive me for the many compliments I have thought but never spoken.

Forgive me for the times I have spoken highly of my spouse to others but have not complimented him directly.

Amen

Passage

So encourage each other and build each other up. 1 THESSALONIANS 5:11

Practice

① Give your spouse one compliment on his appearance right now. Then make it a point to look for things to compliment every day.

② Make a list of all the things your spouse has done this past week. Reflect on the energy, effort, and sacrifice these things took. Thank your partner for doing these things.

③ Write down ten positive character qualities you have discovered about your spouse. In the form of a compliment, share one of these qualities with your spouse every day over the next ten days.

④ When someone compliments your partner in any way, publicly reaffirm the compliment.

RULE ❺
WORK TOGETHER AS A TEAM

MEG AND EDDIE WERE STUCK.

Meg insisted that marriage was hard work—that a couple had to stand together and struggle through a host of difficulties. She believed that challenges were a normal part of any relationship and that they were simply something to overcome.

Eddie thought that if two people loved each other, marriage should be smooth and easy. He believed that difficulties were a sign of crisis and that there should be no problems in a good marriage.

The young couple came to me to find out who was right.

I asked Eddie, "If you have the car of your dreams, what do you do to keep it running smoothly?"

"You change the oil every three thousand miles, rotate the tires, keep your fluids topped off, and make sure you respond quickly when something doesn't sound right."

"Does that take much work?"

"Of course it does," Eddie laughed, "but if you don't take care of the details, you'll pay the price."

"That's the way it is with marriage," I said. "If you want it to run properly you have to take care of it. And that means regular and consistent maintenance."

Eddie sighed, but he heard what I said. During the next month, Eddie stopped reacting negatively when difficulties arose in the marriage and started working to make things better. Several months later, Meg and Eddie came to me again.

"I've been working hard," Eddie said, "but we still seem to be struggling."

That's when we began to talk about the need to work together as a team.

It is so easy for a couple to get out of sync and work against each other. Every couple needs to understand this concept and instead embrace the idea of becoming intimate allies. Allies communicate and defend each other. They coordinate their efforts and help each other out.

Marriage is like a three-legged race: Try to push ahead without your partner's cooperation, and you both fall. Work together, and you both do well.

Not long ago I was watching a great basketball game. In the heat of competition, two teammates went for a rebound and battled against each other for the ball. I felt like yelling, "You're on the same team!" Finally one player realized what they were doing and let go of the ball.

In marriage, you sometimes forget you're on the same team as your spouse. Your spouse is not your enemy or your competitor. The two of you are one. If your partner wins, so do you. If your spouse loses, you do too. Your fates are linked.

It's amazing what can be accomplished in your marriage when you work together. You cover one another's weaknesses and reinforce each other's strengths. When one stumbles, the other helps him up. This is what marriage is all about.

In the fall of 1919, President Woodrow Wilson experienced a nervous breakdown and a cerebral hemorrhage that paralyzed his left side. Realizing that her husband was incapable of performing his presidential duties, his wife stepped in to protect him from the press and coordinate his executive responsibilities. Those who wished to talk to the president had to go through Mrs. Wilson. For the rest of his term, the president relied on his wife to keep everything on an even keel. It wasn't until years later that the public realized how ill the president had been and how Mrs. Wilson had helped her husband by doing all that he could not.

In Genesis, we're told that the two shall become one. That is what marriage is all about. Togetherness becomes "twogetherness" when two "me's" submit to each other and become one "we." As you do this, you become stronger, closer, more efficient, more in sync, less lonely, and less stressed. And as an added bonus, your marriage will become much more enjoyable.

As the two of you work together as a team, there are at least five important factors that need to be present:

Commitment: If two people are not solidly committed to each other, their marriage will sooner or later fall apart. Trust is the foundation of a good marriage, and trust begins with commitment. Each of you needs to know that your spouse is committed to you and your marriage. The traditional marriage vows say, "for better or for worse; for richer or for poorer; in sickness and in health; to love, to honor, and to cherish until death do us part." This is true commitment. Tami and I have a commitment that we won't even use the word *divorce*. We're both totally committed to honesty, faithfulness, and a lifelong love.

Communication: Without communication, any team is in trouble. If both Tami and I know we need a gallon of milk from the local market, but we don't talk about who will pick it up, then we risk having either two gallons of milk or no gallons of milk. It's important that you communicate your thoughts, ideas, plans, and opinions on a regular basis. You also need to communicate your feelings—those joys and fears and frustrations in your heart. Author H. Norman Wright says that communication is the key to a good marriage. Communication forms the connection that allows you to understand each other and grow closer. When communication grows quiet, your relationship will turn cold, distant, and unsatisfying.

Coordination: Without coordination, your marriage will face conflict and tension; you will find yourselves working against each other. Coordination means figuring out a way to work together that uses both partners' talents and abilities. It doesn't mean competing with each other or letting one person do all the work. When your efforts are coordinated, life goes more smoothly and more is accomplished. Several months ago Tami and I redid the floor of our kitchen. We worked as a team—pulling up the old floor, laying down tile, and filling the spaces with mortar. Every time I look at our new floor, I am reminded of what our coordination accomplished. Those who coordinate their efforts can complete plays, finish projects, and create a camaraderie that knits hearts together.

Consideration: Without consideration, feelings are hurt and your dreams slip through your fingers. A lack of consideration is selfishness, and selfish players undermine a team. True teammates show consideration for their partner's feelings, interests, needs, desires, and preferences. Peter tells husbands to "be considerate as you live with your wives, and treat them with respect . . . so that nothing will hinder your prayers" (1 Peter 3:7, NIV). Lack of consideration blocks your wishes, while real consideration ultimately gives you what you want. This works for both husbands and wives. As I am considerate of and sensitive to Tami, she is considerate of and sensitive to me. In fact, what she gives back often far exceeds what I gave her in the first place. When we're considerate with each other, our communication and coordination improve. And so does our marriage.

Clarity: Without clarity of vision, a team has no goal or direction. The players wander aimlessly in circles or slip into that dreaded downward spiral. Dreams give us clarity. They energize us and motivate us and give us hope. Someone once said that if you aim at nothing, you'll probably hit it. Don't let this happen to you. Dream big and dream together. Plan for the future with excitement and anticipation. Robert F. Kennedy once said, "Some men see things as they are and say, 'Why?' But I dream of things that never were and say, 'Why not?'" A couple who is looking in the same direction can walk forward hand in hand with determination and satisfaction. We all need dreams, plus the passion and courage to pursue them. Tami and I have hundreds of dreams: dreams for our marriage, for our children, for our home and community; dreams of places to go, things to do, and memories to make; educational dreams, recreational dreams, and ministry dreams. All of these dreams pull us together as a team, giving our lives a greater purpose and meaning and clarity.

As you and your spouse build and strengthen each other with these five factors, you will find you are truly working together as a team. In doing so, you will also discover that:

Commitment + Communication + Coordination + Consideration + Clarity = Contentment.

On a crisp autumn afternoon my youngest son, who was six or seven at the time, was playing in a soccer game. Suddenly one of his teammates tumbled to the ground. The game continued, but my son did not. He ran to the other boy, knelt beside him, and made sure he was okay. After a few minutes the two boys returned to the game, but in the meantime the opposing team had scored a goal.

"Dusty, why didn't you keep playing?" I asked him later.

"My friend fell down."

"But he was okay, wasn't he?"

"Yes, Dad," he said with a serious look on his face. "But teammates are worried about a lot more than just winning the game."

On that day I was reminded that working together as a team is about a lot more than reaching a goal. Sometimes it involves stepping out of the game and kneeling beside your teammate.

A marriage is hard work, but it is work done together. It is hard work done as the two of you remember that you are both on the same team—covering each other's back, helping each other's play, and sometimes even kneeling at each other's side.

TODAY'S TOOLS

Prayer

Dear God,

Forgive me for the times when marriage has been tough and I have not worked hard enough to make it better. Also, forgive me for all the times I have not worked together with my spouse to improve our situation.

Help me to see my partner as an ally and a teammate, even when we seem to be pulling in different directions.

*Empower me to hold strong to a **commitment** that is total and timeless.*

*Teach me to practice good **communication.***

*Show me all that can be accomplished through the **coordination** of our efforts.*

*Remind me of how **consideration** softens both of our hearts.*

*Encourage me to have a **clarity** of vision that fosters the wonder of dreams and helps those dreams become reality.*

When all is said and done, teach me how to be the sort of teammate you want me to be.

Amen

Passage

Work hard and cheerfully at whatever you do, as though you were working for the Lord rather than for people. COLOSSIANS 3:23

Practice

① Go to a place that holds special memories for both of you, and talk about the following commitments:
  • to never purposefully hurt each other
  • to protect each other's back
  • to be faithful emotionally and sexually
  • to keep promises
  • to be honest
  • to never threaten divorce
  • to love each other all through your lives
② Find a project around your home for the two of you to work on together until completion.
③ Cut out pictures from magazines and catalogues that represent:
  • three "together" dreams for the next five years
  • three "together" dreams for the next ten years
  • three "together" dreams for the next twenty years
  When you are finished, make plans for how you can make these dreams come true.

RULE ❻
MIND YOUR MANNERS

IT ALL ENDED IN THE GROCERY STORE.

Joyce was waiting patiently beside Gary as the cashier rang up their purchases. But Gary couldn't wait. He suddenly swore and pushed past her, accidentally knocking the checkbook from her hand and throwing her off balance. He looked back without a word and started bagging the groceries.

Joyce fumed.

Gary couldn't even say, "Excuse me," or "I'm sorry," or "Are you okay?" and Joyce had had enough. For her, that single incident ended the relationship. It symbolized the accumulation of six years of rudeness. Although Gary had been polite while they dated, once the wedding was over he became a different person.

"He is more polite to strangers than he is to me," Joyce said with a mixture of hurt and anger.

When Joyce demanded that Gary move out of the couple's house, he quickly learned that even in our fast-paced world, concepts like manners and courtesy still have their place. But most of us have gotten lazy. In the book of Ephesians it says, "Do not let any unwholesome talk come out of your mouths" (Ephesians 4:29, NIV). In the following book, the apostle Paul makes a similar appeal: "Whatever happens, conduct yourselves in a manner worthy of the gospel of Christ" (Philippians 1:27, NIV).

In recent years, our culture has become more casual in how we relate to one another, but in that casualness we seem to have forgotten our manners. We don't say "please" and "thank you." We interrupt. We don't open doors for our spouse and we don't let him or her go first. We get loud and pushy. We don't ask or listen. We have become oblivious to the needs of others. And the worst problem of all is that we don't even notice how offensive our lack of manners has become.

If you love your spouse, take a moment to consider your actions. Think about how you speak and act to him, and then ask yourself the following five questions:

1. Are you respectful, or are you rude?
2. Are you polite, or are you inappropriate?
3. Are you mannerly, or are you crude?
4. Are you patient, or are you demanding?
5. Are you courteous, or are you selfish?

By asking these questions, you'll be able to focus on the areas of your life that need some fine-tuning. Henry James, the nineteenth-century American novelist, said this: "Three things in human life are important. The first is to be kind. The second is to be kind. And the third is to be kind." In 1 Corinthians 13, the famous love chapter of the Bible, the apostle Paul agrees: "Love is kind" (1 Corinthians 13:4, NIV).

My mother always told me to mind my manners and be polite. If you are kind and polite to your spouse, she will be kind and polite to you. If you don't mind your manners, the seeds of disrespect are being planted. And sooner or later, those seeds will contaminate even the best-kept field of marriage.

One marriage counselor I know has a unique approach to bringing couples closer together. He asks them to set their dinner table with candlesticks and fine china. He tells them both to dress in their very best. The husband is to shave, splash on cologne, and wear a suit and tie. The wife is to do her hair, put on make-up, and wear her most elegant dress. Then they are to light the candles and eat their meal.

According to the counselor, this simple assignment improves almost every marriage.

Why?

When we're dressed up, we tend to behave better. People are more polite when they look nice and are in a more formal setting. Candlesticks, fine china, and good grooming provide this setting.

When a husband and wife are rude, crude, insensitive, or inattentive toward each other, you know something is wrong. Yet when they treat each other well and show gentleness, patience, thoughtfulness, or caring toward one another, you know their marriage is probably very healthy. You say to yourself, "There is a couple in love." You might even say, "I wish we could be more like that."

Sometimes, in an attempt to improve our relationships, we create a list of all the things our spouse could and should do better. This strategy rarely works. The only thing it accomplishes is to make us more frustrated and discontented. I suggest that you start with yourself. As you become more polite and kindhearted, sooner or later your spouse will notice. (I promise she will.) In time, it will start to rub off on her—probably not as fast as you wish it would, but if you are patient and consistent, things will improve. Unfortunately, most of us get tired and give up too soon. We nag and demand and threaten and decide to give him a little of his own medicine. In doing so, we become just as rude as he is, and things get worse instead of better.

Make a commitment to start with yourself. Start today to be more polite and less demanding, more considerate and less obnoxious, more generous and less hurtful, more attentive and less distracted, more thankful and less selfish. As a psychologist, I call this "positive regard." When you treat your spouse with positive regard, she soon begins to feel better about herself, about you, and about your marriage. Positive regard communicates acceptance, respect, and honor. Good manners do the same thing.

Another great way to mind your manners is to say "I'm sorry." For some reason this seems especially hard for guys. The words are so simple, but we don't say them nearly as often as we should. Good manners demand that you say "I'm sorry" whenever it is needed. Unfortunately, many couples don't recognize when it is needed. So here are twelve times to say "I'm sorry":

1. When you are wrong
2. When you are rude
3. When you are defensive
4. When you are impatient
5. When you are negative
6. When you are hurtful
7. When you are insensitive
8. When you are forgetful
9. When you are confused or confusing
10. When you have neglected something important to the one you love
11. When you have damaged something that was your partner's
12. When you have not said, "I'm sorry" as sincerely or quickly as you should have

These two words are not a cure-all for bad manners, but they certainly don't hurt.

In the southern states they often call good manners "social graces." Ann Platz and Susan Wales, two southern belles who have written a book on etiquette and charm, say that good manners are a way to show our love. When we truly love someone we act a certain way. Being polite is simply an effort to be kind, show respect, and treat others in the way they most desire to be treated. Wales sums it up this way: "Where there is love, there are manners." And let me add this: Where there are good manners, there is the potential for a great marriage.

TODAY'S TOOLS

Prayer

Dear God,

At times I can be so rude and insensitive. I get wrapped up in what I want and how I think life should be without any regard for my spouse's feelings.

Forgive me for my rudeness and bad manners. Forgive me when I am so caught up in myself that I don't even notice my rudeness and bad manners. Forgive me when I try to justify or excuse my bad behavior.

Remind me of the right words at the right time so my words bring my spouse and me closer, rather than creating distance between us.

Assist me in letting no unwholesome words come from my mouth. And when I blow it, give me the grace to apologize quickly and do what needs to be done to repair my foolishness.

Show me how to be kind and patient in the midst of this fast-paced, egocentric world I live in.

Dear God, teach me to mind my manners.

Amen

Passage

Love is patient and kind. Love is not . . . rude. 1 Corinthians 13:4-5

Practice

① Say "please" and "thank you" to your spouse at least three times today.
② Go through the list of "twelve times to say 'I'm sorry,' " and circle the situations where it's hardest for you to say this. Then apologize to your spouse for at least one of those things.
③ Ask your partner what specific things in the area of good manners she would most like you to start practicing. Write them down and then make a commitment to seriously develop those qualities.

RULE ❼
WATCH LESS TV

"WHAT ARE YOU WATCHING?" Tess asked her husband, Matt.

"Nothing."

"But the TV is on and you're sitting in front of it," said Tess.

"It's a stupid show," said Matt.

"What's it about?"

"I don't really know, except that it's worthless."

"Then why are you watching it?"

"I don't know," Matt shrugged. "I guess 'cause there's nothing better to watch."

"So why don't you just turn it off?"

"I probably should, but there might be something better on in twenty minutes."

Tess shook her head and walked away to spend another evening alone while her husband sat in his favorite chair, remote control poised strategically in his hand, his eyes glued to a blur of flashing images.

Television isn't bad, but it can do bad things to your marriage. It can pull you apart and steal precious moments, filling them with irrelevant and sometimes highly questionable material.

One of the problems with television is that it has the ability to hypnotize those who watch it. You know what happens when you sit down and flip on the TV. Soon, you find yourself totally absorbed by what you see and oblivious to what is happening around you.

Your children are fighting.

Your wife is calling you for dinner.

Your sofa has burst into flames.

But you're focused on the game, as your favorite sports team battles neck and neck with an opponent.

Television obsessions come in a variety of flavors: there's the sports fanatic, the sitcom junkie, the history buff, the soap-opera addict, and the news nut. Or maybe you're hooked on medical dramas, lawyer shows, or reality television. Whatever your preference, you're probably watching more TV than you need to watch. Therefore, here are a few rules that might help you to tame your TV habit:

1. Choose ahead of time what you really want to watch, and only turn on the television when that show has started. When the program has ended, turn off the TV before the next show begins.
2. Decide how many hours of TV per day are appropriate for your family. Then discipline yourself to stay within those limits.
3. Don't watch TV alone. Decide that you will only watch programs that you and your spouse both want to see. Sit together on the same couch and watch those shows together. If your spouse really doesn't want to watch something, don't watch it.
4. Talk about what you watch.
5. Find a show that you both enjoy, then once a week set up a date time to watch your special show. Make it a tradition that is fun and romantic.

Television is consuming and must be controlled, or it will control you.

Television draws you in and won't let you go. It demands your attention and resents competition. My wife and I have found a substitute, however. It's music. Music is not so demanding. It is equally content to shape your mood or merely set the atmosphere, allowing you to leave the room and return whenever you wish. It is more social than the television since it allows you to talk over it and through it. Music can draw a couple together, and the right music at the right time can reinforce a bond that:

intensifies intimacy
deepens connectedness
builds priceless memories

Someone once said that music is the soundtrack of our lives. Therefore, find music that touches you both, and then allow your home to overflow with sounds that nurture and refresh your soul. Fill your mornings with up-lifting and lively music. In the evening listen to relaxing melodies. Keep a collection of your favorite romantic songs in your bedroom. When inspiring music is playing, you'll be less likely to turn on the television.

As you learn to appreciate music together, look for songs or even one song that you both can call "our song." Over the course of our marriage, Tami and I have collected at least seven songs that we call "ours." Each has a different story and each holds certain magic. Each is sublimely special.

Tami and I have many songs, but one of my favorites is "Have I Told You Lately (That I Love You)?" written by Van Morrison. The first time Tami and I heard this powerful ballad, it was five o'clock in the morning and I was rushing Tami to the hospital for the birth of our second child. As the words flowed from the radio, the two of us looked at each other; it was as if this song had been written just for us. It was definitely "our song."

Now, ten years later, the song is still just as powerful as it was that clear June morning when we first heard it. When Tami catches "our song" during the day, she'll call me and place the telephone receiver to the radio. During those moments, we're able to share our love in a unique and intimate way.

Several years ago, we were strolling through a small shop in Cannon Beach, Oregon, when we heard one of our songs. Suddenly the shopkeeper and the other tourists faded from our awareness. We held each other's hands and kissed. At that moment nothing in the universe existed except the two of us, our love, and "our song."

If you don't have at least one special song, you are missing out on something wonderful. Think back to the songs that were meaningful during your courtship and marriage. Christen one of them as "our song," and then add others as they touch your heart. Even when we go on vacations we take a CD player along with at least one of "our songs." That way we're never far from the wonderful memories that add to the romance and intimacy of our love.

TODAY'S TOOLS

Prayer

Dear God,

Keep me from becoming so distracted by TV that it steals my time—time that would be much better spent connecting with my spouse.

Forgive me for the times I have not listened to or shown my love for my spouse because I was too consumed by a program that means nothing in the light of eternity.

When I do watch TV, show me how to do it in a wise and responsible way that doesn't build walls but instead builds a bond that can't be broken.

Fill my marriage with beautiful music—positive, exciting, romantic music. And when the sad songs come, draw us into each other's arms.

Send us special music that touches our hearts and strengthens our love. Give us a song that can truly be "our song."

Amen

Passage

Fix your thoughts on what is true and honorable and right. Think about things that are pure and lovely and admirable. Think about things that are excellent and worthy of praise. PHILIPPIANS 4:8

Practice

① Sit down with your spouse and read the five TV rules together. Determine to put each rule into practice for one week. After the five weeks are over, talk about the rules you'd like to try for a full year.

② Find some relaxing music that you both like, and play it at the end of the day as you both enjoy the closeness of each other's company.

③ Think back over all the meaningful songs you've heard in the course of your relationship. Or find songs that express your thoughts or feelings about each other. Collect these songs and burn them onto a CD or record them on a tape as a special gift to your spouse.

RULE ⑧
FIND TIME FOR FUN

WHEN TWO PEOPLE FIRST MEET, they're often drawn to one another by the fun they have when they're together. When Tami and I were getting to know each other we laughed and played. We flew kites and swam rivers and took hikes. Everything from walking in the rain to watching a sunset was an adventure. We went to plays and concerts and parks. We made sand castles and gingerbread houses and had romantic dinners.

Before marriage, most couples know how to have fun. But once they get married, the stresses of life build. There are bills to pay and meetings to attend and responsibilities to meet; before you know it, life becomes more serious. Then come a house or children and unforeseen difficulties. Soon all the pressures of life begin to squeeze out much of the fun you once shared. There just isn't the time, energy, or money to have as much fun as you once had.

Far too often, married couples have forgotten how to really let loose and have fun. Several years ago I was teaching a class on marriage to seminary students. When I started talking about the importance of fun and how every married couple needs to set aside chunks of time to play, the students looked at me with blank stares.

"When was the last time you and your spouse spent the day just having fun?" I asked.

The class was silent for several moments until finally a lone student raised his hand and said, "I'm not sure how this is relevant to marriage."

The class nodded in agreement.

"We're all very busy," the student continued. "We have so many important things to do and not enough hours in the day to do them. We can't afford to waste our time."

My heart sank.

These students, so bright and promising, were sabotaging their marriages and they didn't even see it. When a couple plays and laughs together, they are creating an emotional connection that will be necessary to help them get through the conflicts and crises of marriage. As Dave and Claudia Arp, founders of Marriage Alive, say, "Having fun is serious business."

Sit down with your spouse and talk about having fun.
Discuss it.
Plan it.
Budget it.
Do it.

Playfulness helps you relax, and when you relax, you'll find that you're able to relate to one another in a more positive manner. When the busyness and pressures of life get to you, your stress level builds. When you are stressed, you become irritable, impatient, and negative. Having fun relieves stress and builds great memories.

Some of the best memories Tami and I have are of times when we were having fun. We've had great times hiking and snorkeling and exploring places both close to home and far away. Even as I'm writing these words

Tami and I are sitting beside a pool on the Oregon coast, watching our three kids laugh and play in the water. What a great time. What a great memory.

Unfortunately, some people associate fun and playfulness with immaturity. They seem to think that fun is something you outgrow. I hope I never outgrow playfulness, joy, and laughter. Tami and I love having fun with our kids and friends.

Several years ago, on a hot August afternoon, our neighborhood had a great water fight. We got together with our kids and stretched our garden hoses into the street. There were water guns and water buckets and water balloons. The goal? To get as wet as possible and to have fun. It was a wonderful afternoon. Then a neighbor drove by wearing a three-piece suit and a serious grimace. His look seemed to say, "What in the world are you doing? Grow up and act like adults. You shouldn't be having that much fun."

So what did we do?

Sadly enough, we allowed that one look to put an end to our fun. We rolled up the hoses, put away the buckets, and went into our houses to act like adults are supposed to act. What should we have done? We should have gone right on playing together and building relationships with one another. Because we allowed our neighbor to put an end to our fun, we missed a great opportunity to draw closer. So relax and don't let anything or anybody keep you from having fun.

One of the things that frequently blocks a couple from fun is that neither person is quite sure what to do. Here's an easy way to get started. Get a pencil and paper, and sit down with your spouse. Make a list of all the fun things that come to your mind. I'm sure there are plenty of times when you've both said, "Someday I'd like to do that." Write them down. Think of things you've already done and really enjoyed. If you've ever thought about something and said, "Someday I'd like to do that again," add that to your list. Here are a few suggestions to get you started:

1. Bake cookies together.
2. Plan out your dream vacation.
3. Dance in your living room.
4. Go on a hike.
5. Play your favorite board game.
6. Rent a funny video.
7. Visit a local amusement park.
8. Pack up a picnic lunch.
9. Read Dr. Seuss books aloud to each other.
10. Have a water fight with your neighbors.

Life offers us hundreds of adventures. Write them down and keep your list handy. When you discover something new, add it to your list. Then toward the beginning of each month pull out your list and schedule a time to do at least one thing before the end of the month.

If you're still stuck and not sure what to do for fun, consider the simple pleasure of laughing. Every couple needs to laugh together. Lighten up and develop a good sense of humor. A healthy couple uses humor to break up tension, move closer together, build great memories, and have more fun. No matter how difficult a situation, laughter can help you get through it. During one of the most stressful times of our marriage, I was given a subscription to *Reader's Digest*. At the end of a hard day Tami and I would lie in bed, reading the humor sections. Before long one of us would start laughing, then the other would join in. Soon we were both laughing so hard that all the cares of life seemed to disappear.

Laughter is good medicine. It heals many a hurt and will strengthen your marriage! When life is heavy, a sense of humor can make things seem lighter. Proverbs says, "The cheerful heart has a continual feast" (Proverbs 15:15, NIV). A smile can make everything appear more positive. Laughter makes you feel better; it reduces stress and pushes away depression. It is also contagious. Try this test: Look over at your partner and smile (or giggle, if you're feeling brave). I'll bet your partner smiles (or giggles) in response.

If you want a great marriage, make a commitment to have some fun. Be responsible and do what needs to be done, but wear a smile. Develop a cheerful heart and a sense of humor. Play to your heart's content and laugh until your sides hurt. Do what you did when you first met each other and your love was fresh.

TODAY'S TOOLS

Prayer

Dear God,

Thank you for creating a world that includes time for fun and play and laughter.

Teach us to have more fun. Forgive us for all the times we take life too seriously, letting the trials and troubles of each day blind us to the excitement and joy that surround us.

Help us to find the balance between hard work and solid play. Remind us that for six days you created, and on the seventh day you rested. Show us how to rest and relax and play.

Place in our hearts a sparkling laughter that can lighten the heaviest burden. Give us a contagious enthusiasm for all that is good and right and pure. Let our laughter lift each other up. Let it spread beyond ourselves to those with whom we come in contact, lifting their spirits and pointing them to the source of all hope.

Return us to that time in our marriage when fun and play and laughter seemed so natural.

Amen

Passage

There is a time for everything, a season for every activity under heaven. . . . A time to cry and a time to laugh. A time to grieve and a time to dance. Ecclesiastes 3:1, 4

Practice

① Make a list of ten things you did before you were married that were fun. Reminisce with your spouse about these, and schedule time together to do one thing on your list sometime in the next week.

② If you are experiencing stress and difficulty in your life right now, talk with your spouse about the positive (or humorous) side of your situation. Pray together and thank God that he gives the good with the bad.

③ Rent a comedy video or find a book of humorous stories, then sit together on your sofa and let yourselves laugh and laugh and laugh.

DO THE LITTLE THINGS

"ISN'T IT BEAUTIFUL?" asked Jack excitedly as the deliverymen unloaded the superdeluxe, shiny new washing machine into the garage.

"Yes," said Meagan, "but it's so big."

"I know, isn't it great?"

"But it looks so complicated and expensive."

"It's the top of the line," said Jack, "the very best they had."

"I appreciate it, but all I really wanted was an ordinary, everyday washing machine."

One of the mistakes we guys often make is thinking "the bigger, the better." Meanwhile, our wives simply want to know that we care about them. When it comes to showing affection, a single rose can be as powerful as a dozen, and dessert at a local café can be as treasured as a five-course dinner at the most elegant restaurant in town.

Big plans can be nice, but more often, it's the little things that count the most. John Gottman, a top researcher in the area of marital satisfaction, says it's the "little movements toward our spouse that increase our contentment with each other. It is the smile, the opening of a door, the backrub, the kiss on the cheek, the kind word, or the gift of their favorite ice cream."

Some people are givers, and some are takers. Tami is definitely a giver and she knows how to give in a hundred little ways. She leaves romantic notes and rich chocolate in my suitcase when I have to travel out of town. She fixes my favorite meals when she knows my stress level is high. She offers words of encouragement whenever she can. She snuggles up beside me and puts her arms around me and whispers that she loves me. Each little thing she does is a sparkling treasure; by itself it may be small, but as the little things accumulate, I realize that I'm a very wealthy man.

In the true story *A Severe Mercy* by Sheldon Vanauken, the author writes about a code of chivalry he shared with his wife. The code, which involved a commitment to focus on the small things, was symbolized by a simple glass of water. Whenever Sheldon asked for a glass of water, his wife would, without hesitation or question, fulfill the request. And whenever his wife asked for a glass of water, Sheldon did the same. There are few things in this world as refreshing as a tall glass of ice-cold water. When I go to sleep I like some cold water next to my bed, in case I get thirsty. Although I never said anything about the water to Tami, she noticed my pattern after a while. And every night for the past ten years, Tami has brought a tall glass of ice and water to the bedroom. It's one more example of doing the little things. Every time I see that glass I am reminded of how much Tami loves me.

Years ago I was told that the definition of a gift is giving someone what they want, while the definition of a present is giving someone something you want them to have. In the Old Testament, Jonathan told David, "Whatever you want me to do, I'll do for you" (1 Samuel 20:4, NIV). What a gift! I want to learn how to give that generously, whether it involves energy, time, words, or tangible gifts. To do this, I need to learn what my wife likes and wants. In some ways, I need to commit myself to being an expert on my wife. You can do the same thing with your spouse:

What things are important to him?
What brings her joy?

What are his hobbies and interests?

What has she always wanted?

What makes him smile?

What does she collect?

What would he appreciate most?

What would make her life easier?

Be proactive. Look for ways you can do the little things for your spouse every single day. Be creative. Be personal. Be generous. Tami likes shoulder rubs, so several times a week I pull out the massage oil and do my best to work the tension out of her shoulders. Tami also loves flowers, especially freesia, roses, and daffodils. So periodically I bring home flowers to brighten her day. All of these little things are messages that I love her, I'm thinking of her, and she truly is the most important person in my life. You can never give too many of these messages.

I try to keep a mental list of what makes Tami smile. She likes chocolate truffles, bubble baths, action-packed movies, shopping at the mall, fancy tea-pots, Mary Higgins Clark mysteries, and mint-chocolate-chip ice cream. Tami also likes coffee, but she isn't drawn to your normal, everyday, plain coffee. She wants something that is uniquely hers. After several months of mental rehearsal I could finally order her favorite at the local coffee shop. She was quite impressed when I told the clerk my wife wanted a "single decaf white chocolate mint mocha skinny with two beans on top." A few months later she switched favorites. Now she wants a "single decaf vanilla latte skinny with no beans." No matter how often she changes her mind, I want to get her what she really wants.

I want to do the little things for Tami, and that often means paying attention to the details and then trying hard to remember them. I used to trust my memory, but lately I've given up. Now I have a piece of paper neatly folded and tucked in my wallet. I write down things she mentions that she likes as well as her clothing sizes and her most recent choice of beverage at the coffee shop. I've found that the more I do little things for Tami, the more she does for me. All I do for her returns to me tenfold. As we do for each other, our love and appreciation grow and grow. And over time, the little things add up.

I know a couple who placed all their change in a jar at the end of each day. As the years passed they accumulated many jars of change. After fifteen years, they cashed in all the change, and to their surprise they had saved enough to take a second honeymoon to Hawaii. Pennies, nickels, dimes, and quarters add up. So do the good deeds. They soften the hard edges of life and compensate for our foolish mistakes. They build treasured memories and assure a positive relationship that will last "till death do us part."

TODAY'S TOOLS

Prayer

Dear God,

When I am tempted to get wrapped up in myself, help me to look beyond my own wants and wishes and needs. Forgive me for my selfishness.

Give me the desire to make my beloved smile by giving generously the little things of life that might require my time, energy, money, and planning.

Remind me that it truly is better to give than to receive.

Show me how to give freely and cheerfully and spontaneously. Make me more of a giver and less of a taker.

Teach me to give like you give. Thank you for your abundant gifts and all the little ways you bring beauty, comfort, and wonder into my life.

Inspire me to do the little things each day that show my spouse that I love him and appreciate all he has given me.

Amen

Passage

Do for others what you would like them to do for you. MATTHEW 7:12

Practice

① Find something special you can do for your spouse one day this week. It's okay to start simple. Does she like coffee in the morning? Start it brewing while she's in the shower. Does he like a certain magazine? Make an effort to pick up a copy for him.

② Take a few minutes and write down as many of your spouse's preferences or special interests as you can think of. If you're not in the habit of observing your spouse, you may be surprised at how few details you know! Keep the list in an accessible place and update it as you learn more about your husband or wife.

③ Using the ideas you came up with earlier, make a list of twenty little gifts (under $10) that you think your spouse might like. Give him one of these gifts each week for the next twenty weeks.

④ Watch other couples to see what little things they do for one another. Write down these ideas and then set aside a special day when you try as many of them as possible within a twenty-four-hour period.

RULE ❿
CELEBRATE THE "TOP FIVE"

"I'M IN TROUBLE," said Nate, a thirty-something man in a gray Nike tank top.

"What kind of trouble?" I asked.

"My wife won't talk to me and I'm sleeping on the sofa."

"So, what did you do that hurt or offended Cheryl?" I asked.

"Yesterday was her thirtieth birthday, and I forgot it," Nate said sheepishly. "But that's not all. Our wedding anniversary is on the same day as her birthday, and I forgot that, too."

Nate knew he had blown it, and he genuinely regretted his failure. So that afternoon he bought thirty different birthday cards and thirty different anniversary cards. He wrote "I love you," and "Please forgive me" on each one. Then he carefully placed them throughout the house with several hundred chocolate kisses.

When Cheryl arrived home from work, she was both surprised and impressed by Nate's effort. But the best was yet to come! That night when she slipped into bed she found one more card. Inside it was a handwritten poem telling Cheryl thirty reasons she was the best wife in the world, plus two airline tickets to Hawaii for a second honeymoon.

Tears streamed down Cheryl's face as she turned to Nate. "I just wanted to know I was special. Yesterday when you didn't even acknowledge two of the most important days of the year, I felt like nothing. But today you've made up for it. Thank you for showing me that you really care."

Celebrations are a way of saying:

"I love you."
"You are special!"
"I'm glad I married you."
"You are appreciated."
"Thank you!"

We all know we ought to be saying these words every day of the year, but it's easy to get distracted and wrapped up in the busyness of life. So there are special days set aside on your calendar for these messages. Yet too often we don't take full advantage of these invaluable opportunities to strengthen our marriages.

I call these opportunities the "Top Five," a handful of holidays when you ought to be especially proactive about your love. You probably know what these celebrations are, but let me remind you anyway:

Christmas
Valentine's Day
Your wedding anniversary
Your spouse's birthday
Mother's/Father's Day

Maybe your list looks a little different. At any rate, these days give you chances to be a hero. If you put some time and effort into each of these, I guarantee your spouse will draw closer to you. Last Sunday was Father's Day and I awoke early to the smell of blueberry pancakes (my favorite). I walked downstairs to the kitchen, still rubbing the sleep from my eyes, to find a wonderful breakfast in my honor, three cards, five gifts, and a wife who loves me.

These days of celebration are chances to be generous and giving. One of the easiest things you can do is give your spouse a card. Whenever Tami drives past a card store, she says she's inexplicably drawn into it, and the longer she stays inside, the broader her smile. I, on the other hand, will do almost anything to avoid these stores. Spending time browsing through cards and gift wrap is certainly not my idea of having fun. However, I know that if I give Tami a card, it will have a powerful and romantic impact on our relationship. Tami has taught me the fine art of giving a card:

1. Read it.
2. Write a note on it.
3. Mail it.

These three simple actions will greatly increase the impact of your card.

Everyone loves gifts, but some of us are better at receiving than giving. On each of the "Top Five" holidays, you must give your partner a special gift. There are no excuses, justifications, or explanations acceptable. I realize that some years are tough, and you might think it's better not to exchange gifts on a particular Christmas or anniversary. This is a big mistake! You should *never* miss an opportunity to boost your marriage. Besides, there are lots of gifts you can give that cost little or no money. One anniversary Tami gave me a small book she had made with coupons in it like "Present this for a fifteen-minute back rub," or "This coupon is good for one romantic date." It was a wonderful gift, and it didn't cost a penny. Be creative and you might be amazed at what other inexpensive gifts you can come up with. In fact, it's often the homemade gift that means the most because your spouse knows you put time and effort into it.

Finally, try to make each of the "Top Five" holidays memorable. Do something extra to make these special days truly unique. Several years ago on Valentine's Day, Tami turned off all the lights and filled our house with candles. On our fifteenth wedding anniversary, I took Tami to an exotic restaurant overlooking the Pacific Ocean and we exchanged gifts at sunset. For Tami's birthday we are going camping (which she loves), and for my next birthday we are going to Mexico (which I love). We try to create positive, romantic memories with each of these celebrations. Then as we think back on years gone by, we can smile at the fullness of our love expressed by a lifetime of special days.

So celebrate each of the "Top Five" in a big way. But don't let yourself be limited by only five days each year, when you still have another 360 chances to show your love. Surprise your spouse by sending a card, giving a gift, or creating a wonderful memory for no particular reason other than to say, "You are special and I am so thankful you are mine."

TODAY'S TOOLS

Prayer

Dear God,

Teach me to be creative in showing my spouse how important he is to me.

On Christmas help me to give as generously as you have given to me.

On Valentine's Day help me to model the true meaning of love in an extraordinary way.

On our anniversary help me to show my appreciation for all the positive things my beloved has done and said and attempted during our marriage.

On his birthday help me to honor him specifically and selflessly for being who he is.

On Mother's Day or Father's Day help me to applaud the way she or he has sacrificially loved, nurtured, protected, and taught our children.

In the midst of my hectic schedule remind me to create a wonderful memory for the special partner you have so graciously given to me.

Amen

Passage

Love each other with genuine affection, and take delight in honoring each other. ROMANS 12:10

Practice

① Talk to your spouse about the "Top Five" and ask how she would most enjoy spending each one. Take careful notes about what you might do in the future.

② Sit down and make cards for the next two special days. In each card write at least a few lines expressing your love. Save each card until a few days before the holiday is celebrated, then mail it.

③ Make plans for the very next of the "Top Five" on the calendar. Decide on a gift to give, something nice to do, and other individual touches you can add to make the day extraspecial.

RULE ⑪
THINK POSITIVE

"I THINK I LOVE HIM," said Celine about Nick, whom she had met six months earlier at a friend's party. "We have similar interests and backgrounds and beliefs. He's a great guy. The only problem is his negativity. He is a glass-half-empty sort of person, and it drives me crazy."

"How serious are you about Nick?" I asked.

"We've talked about marriage, but unless his attitude gets more positive I can't make a commitment."

Celine broke up with Nick three weeks later. She recognized that negativity kills love. It can quickly sour a marriage. In Celine and Nick's case it soured things before they even said "I do."

Negativity is devastating. It sucks the life out of a marriage and can even lead to divorce. Although negativity does cross gender lines, I've found that men comment more on their wives' negativity than the other way around. Wives tend to point out their husbands' insensitivity, stubbornness, and silence, but husbands usually stick to negativity when complaining about their wives. I've counseled many men who sit in my office and say things like:

"Nothing will make her happy."

"No matter what I do, it's not good enough."

"If everything I do is wrong, why try?"

You must understand that most guys truly want to please their wives, but if they're regularly confronted with negativity, sooner or later they give up. They stop disciplining the children, initiating sex, or talking to their wives altogether because they've simply faced too many negative responses.

Negative words or actions can leave deep scars. Even when the negativity is subtle, it still stings. In fact, research shows that it takes eight positives to make up for a single negative. So if you put down your husband in frustration, you'll need to compliment him eight times to make things even.

Negativity is a tough habit to break, too. There are so many ways you can be negative toward your spouse. You can be critical, bitter, argumentative, grumpy, sarcastic, short-tempered, passive-aggressive, unresponsive, impatient, cynical, complaining, unhappy, resistant, sharp, nagging, ignoring, defensive, or frustrated. And these are just a few. Some of you are very skilled at one or two of the negative behaviors on the above list. Maybe this is due to your personality, your genetics, or your childhood, but you don't have to let it continue. Starting today, you can confront your negative patterns and create something more positive.

Stress is a major factor that can steal your ability to be positive. Of all the people who show up at my office, about 80 percent struggle with some sort of stress reaction. Their stress might come from work, finances, family, friends, or even their love life. But whatever its source, stress has a way of making life miserable. Among other symptoms of stress, three of the most common are:

impatience
irritability
intolerance of things you would normally ignore

If you find some productive ways to manage your stress, you'll probably begin to see a decrease in your negativity. When you start to feel over-whelmed, try a few of the following ideas:

Take a break.
Go for a walk.
Call a friend.
Read a book or magazine.
Write in a journal.
Relax in a bathtub.
Exercise.
Count your blessings.

Another way to decrease your negativity is to consider your frame of mind. Dr. David Burns, in his book *Feeling Good*, suggests that people become negative as a result of cognitive distortions. These include:

Overgeneralization: This occurs when you see one isolated negative as a never-ending pattern of darkness.

Mental filtering: You do this when you pick out a single negative detail and dwell on it exclusively until your entire focus becomes absorbed by that one small detail.

Disqualifying the positive: This occurs when you reject positive experiences by insisting they don't count for some reason or another.

Magnification and minimization: You do this if you exaggerate the importance of negative things and shrink the importance of the positive.

If you see yourself in any of these examples, you can start today to reverse this way of thinking. As you recognize these patterns and challenge these cognitive distortions, you'll be more apt to think positive.

But thinking positive isn't just about avoiding stress or cognitive distortions; it requires you to focus on the best qualities of life. In his letter to the Philippians, Paul writes that he has learned how to be content regardless of the circumstances (Philippians 4:11, NIV). The key is focus. He says to fix your thoughts on whatever is true, noble, right, pure, lovely, admirable, excellent, and praiseworthy (Philippians 4:8, NIV). In any marriage there are going to be disappointments, hurts, and frustrations. If you focus on these, I guarantee you will become more negative. But there are also a lot of good things to focus on—things like the eight qualities that Paul mentions (listed above). If you focus on these, you can't help but be positive.

In 1999, the movie *Life Is Beautiful* won three Academy Awards and was nominated for Best Picture of the Year. This movie tells the story of Guido, a charming but bumbling waiter with a wife whom he adores and a small son for whom he would do anything. But Guido is Jewish, and being Jewish is a crime in Nazi-influenced Italy during World War II. So Guido and his beloved family are forced into a boxcar and hauled to a concentration camp. The place is hard and dirty, the food is sparse, and the guards are cruel. In the midst of all this pain and degradation and death, Guido keeps a positive attitude. Somehow, he's able to smile and joke and encourage his little family in the worst of circumstances. He has every reason in the world to be negative, but he refuses.

If Guido can be positive, so can you. The bottom line? We're attracted to positive people and we tend to avoid those who are negative. Right now, make an effort to smile and joke and encourage your spouse. It will make you more attractive and you might be surprised at how it can make the most difficult situation beautiful. As the brilliant Sunday comic philosopher Ziggy once said, "You can either complain that rose bushes have thorns—or rejoice that thorn bushes have roses."

TODAY'S TOOLS

Prayer

Dear God,

Life is sometimes hard, but you are always good. Circumstances are sometimes overwhelming, but you are always in control. Marriage is sometimes difficult, but you always provide strength and wisdom and hope.

Teach me to be content in whatever situation I find myself.

Help me not to let the stress of each day make me negative.

Show me ways to correct my negative thinking so it does not steal my joy.

Forgive me for all the times I have let a negative attitude get the best of me. Forgive me for the times I have let my negativity hurt or discourage those whom I love the most.

Remind me of all that is true, noble, right, pure, lovely, admirable, excellent, and praiseworthy about my circumstances and my spouse.

Thank you for giving me these positives to lift my spirit.

Amen

Passage

No matter what happens, always be thankful, for this is God's will for you who belong to Christ Jesus. 1 THESSALONIANS 5:18

Practice

① Talk to your spouse about the times in your marriage when you've been the most negative. What triggered your negative attitude? How can you avoid those triggers in the future? With your spouse, explore ways to turn your attitude toward the positive.

② Agree to play a "positive-building" game with your partner. Each time either of you says *anything* negative about *anything*, that person must put a quarter in his own personal negative jar. When the jar is full, his spouse gets to decide how to spend the money.

③ Look at the four negative distortions and determine which one you struggle with most often. Then ask your spouse to help you find something positive to say each time he hears you fall into an attitude of negativity.

④ Make it a goal to come up with twenty-five positive things in your life. Do you have a job you enjoy? Have you read a great book lately? Did you have a great game of catch with your kids today? If you do this every day for one full month, you'll be amazed at how much more positively you'll see the world.

RULE ⑫
FIGHT FAIR

TAMI AND I LOVE CHRISTMAS. The lights, the tree, the traditions, and ultimately the meaning behind this holiday combine to make this season something wonderful. Each Christmas Eve we gather around the tree to sing carols, read of Christ's birth, and open a host of brightly wrapped packages.

On one particular Christmas Eve all went well until Tami opened a present from her new friend Liz. Liz was a kindhearted, widowed lady who had recently moved into the neighborhood. Tami had invited her over to our home several times for coffee, and Liz had noticed that we had very few things hung on the walls of our family room. So Liz had made Tami the most "unique" painting I had ever seen. When Tami opened the gift we both chuckled, but then the laughter stopped. Pinned to this picture was a note.

"Thank you for your love. I wanted to make something special for your beautiful home, so I've spent the last few months on this landscape. It should look magnificent in your family room above the sofa."

When I read the note my immediate thought was, *There's no way we can hang that painting in our living room!*

But late that night, around midnight, Tami hammered a nail into our family-room wall and hung Liz's landscape.

"What do you think?" she asked.

"I don't want that painting in our house. Don't you think it's one of the ugliest things you've ever seen?"

"It is ugly," Tami agreed. "But Liz is a friend, and I don't want to hurt her feelings."

"Don't you care about *my* feelings? I can't stand that picture, and I think we should get rid of it. It ruins the look of the whole family room."

"Friendship should be more important than how something looks," Tami said.

"But if Liz was a real friend, she never would have given you such an ugly gift."

For the next two hours we fought over Liz's gift. The longer we fought, the more heated and irrational we became. We both dug in our heels and neither of us would admit that the other might have a valid point.

Years later I think back on this fight and realize how stupid it was. Most fights are over foolish little things that in the long haul don't amount to a hill of beans. It's so easy to get caught up in the heat of the battle. In the midst of a disagreement, the issues become so important that we're often willing to stand our ground no matter what. My Grandma Blanche used to say, "What difference will it make in ten years?" With most fights you might also ask, "What difference will it make in one year?" or maybe even "What difference will it make in one month?"

Every couple fights. Some couples fight frequently; others only disagree every once in a while. Some battle with silence; others are loud. Some explode and then it's over; others pick and complain for years. I find that a person's fighting style often resembles that of an animal. Take a look at the following list and see what animal you're most like.

A turtle: You withdraw inside yourself.

A deer: You get away as fast as you can.

A shark: You go for blood.

A donkey: You stand your ground and don't budge.

A chameleon: You give them whatever they want.

An elephant: You give in, but you never forget.

Whatever your style, it's important that you learn how to fight fair. If you don't learn this, you will leave a trail of hurt, anger, disrespect, fear, disappointment, and unresolved conflict behind you. If you learn how to fight fair you will understand your spouse better, and in the end you will find yourself growing closer rather than more distant.

Here are seven crucial principles to fighting fair:

1. **Choose the right time and place.** Most of my fights with Tami have occurred when one or both of us are either tired, hungry, or stressed. These are not good times to fight because it's so easy to become irrational in these situations. It's also important to try not to fight in public or in front of the kids. Conflicts in public bring unneeded embarrassment or humiliation, while conflicts in front of your children can undermine your sense of parental unity and their sense of security.

2. **Show respect.** Watch your volume; yelling can be intimidating. Besides, when the volume level rises, a fight can easily escalate and get out of control. You also need to choose your words carefully; putting your spouse down or calling him names will rarely result in anything positive. The goal in a conflict is to attack the problem, not the person.

3. **Deal with only one issue at a time.** Too often couples skip from one issue to the next without resolving anything. In the midst of a disagreement it's so easy to get off track. One topic leads to another

and soon you have no idea where you started. Promise each other that you will stay on the original issue until you have it resolved.

4. **Stay in the present.** It is hard enough to fight about things in the here and now, but when you start focusing on what happened a month or even a day ago, things can really get complicated. Most people think they have great memories, but that's not the truth. Couples come to me all the time with battles over the past. She remembers it one way and he remembers it another way. In reality, they're probably both wrong. The more time that elapses from an event, the more potential there is for distortion, reinterpretation, and just plain forgetfulness. So try your best to stick to the present and don't argue over the past.

5. **Never interrupt.** It can be so frustrating when you're trying to explain a point and your spouse won't let you finish. To solve this problem, try the "3+3 rule." Start by flipping a coin to determine who goes first. The first person gets to talk for three minutes with absolutely no interruptions while the other person gives his undivided attention. At the end of three minutes, the second person gets equal time. If you both agree there is still more to say, you can always agree to another "3+3." The main point is to listen and not to interrupt.

6. **End with resolution.** I am amazed at how many couples have had ongoing fights and are no closer to resolution than when they began. Remember that the purpose of a marital conflict is to resolve something, not to win. Here are three potential resolutions:

Accommodation: You are willing to change.
Acceptance: You realize your spouse won't or can't change.
Compromise: You are both willing to change.

Resolutions are not always easy, and sometimes you have to try a short-term resolution to see how it fits. Other times you simply have to resolve to meet again to discuss your issues further.

7. **Always make up after a fight.** Often you have to apologize before you can make up. During any fight, things are said or done that aren't in the best interest of the relationship. Apologize for these and then be ready to reconnect. When Tami and I were first married she would say she didn't mind a periodic fight because the making up was so good. After every fight, make it a point to do something special—go on a date, kiss, take a walk, make love, hold hands, pray, or enjoy a romantic meal. Whatever you do, make sure you reconnect and reaffirm your love.

Every couple fights, but fights don't have to be negative. Because God created each of you out of an individual and unique mold, it's only natural that you're going to approach life from different perspectives. This is going to create friction. You don't always have to agree in order to have a great marriage. Positive fights can teach you a lot about each other. As you learn how to fight fair, your respect and appreciation for each other will grow. In the process, you will build a relationship that can last as long as you both shall live.

TODAY'S TOOLS

Prayer

Dear God,
When my beloved and I disagree, help me to fight fair.
Forgive me for the times I get so wrapped up in winning that I forget about my

spouse's feelings, priorities, or needs. Forgive me for my selfishness, my insensitivity, and my stubbornness.

Show me how to fight with respect.

Remind me that you are more concerned with how I fight than with if I am right. Empower me to show your love, peace, patience, and gentleness in the midst of each conflict.

Teach me how to resolve every fight graciously. Soften my heart and open my eyes to what will be best for both me and my spouse.

Thank you for putting up with my foolish, trivial fights, and help me to respond more maturely next time.

Amen

Passage

Never pay back evil for evil to anyone. Do things in such a way that everyone can see you are honorable. ROMANS 12:17

Practice

① Sit down with your spouse and determine each of your fight styles. Are you a turtle, a deer, a shark, a donkey, a chameleon, an elephant, or some other animal?

② Determine which of the seven principles to fighting fair, listed in this chapter, is the most difficult for you. Go to your partner and apologize for the times you have struggled with this. Then discuss how you both might improve in this area.

③ Consider any unresolved conflicts you might currently have with your spouse. Commit yourself to resolving these difficulties today in a way that will respect your spouse and honor God. If this is not possible, contact a pastor or counselor or some competent third party who can help you.

RULE ⓭
FORGIVE

"HOW LONG HAVE YOU KNOWN your marriage was in trouble?"

"Sixteen years," Sandy spoke quickly.

"What have you done to improve your situation?"

"Nothing."

"Why?" I asked.

"I thought things would improve by themselves," she said. "But they have only gotten worse."

In every marriage, there are times you hurt each other. You might say or do something stupid. You might be insensitive or rude. You might betray your spouse's trust or trample her emotions. You may fail to defend, protect, honor, or love your partner. There are hundreds of ways to hurt each other. Sometimes you are keenly aware of what you have done. Other times your spouse suffers in silence while you naively move along, oblivious to the hurt you've left behind.

A marriage is like a dance. No matter how careful you are, periodically you're going to step on your partner's feet. Some people have sensitive feet and some have tough feet, but hurts still happen. If you step on a foot, it's important to seek forgiveness. If you have been stepped on, it's best for you and your marriage if you grant forgiveness. Without forgiveness, the hurts build and the dance stops. Forgiveness allows you to reconnect in a positive way and dance once more.

Forgiveness is not always easy, but it is necessary. You seek forgiveness because you love your spouse and you don't want to cause pain. You grant forgiveness because you realize there have been times you have been forgiven and there will be times in the future you will need to be forgiven once more.

Since none of us is a perfect husband or wife, we're bound to find ourselves in plenty of situations that require forgiveness. This involves swallowing your pride and taking responsibility for what you did, even if you did it unwittingly. I knew a man named Russ who had been married two years and insisted that if you didn't hurt your spouse on purpose it didn't count. His wife said he was wrong. I had to agree with his wife. Stepping on someone's feet causes pain whether you did it on purpose or not.

If you're serious about showing love to your spouse, you will seek forgiveness with every offense. This begins by acknowledging what you have done. Don't justify the offense or come up with excuses. That will just make the situation worse. Even if you feel like your spouse was responsible for 90 percent of the problem, you must take responsibility for your part. Then accept that you have hurt the one you love. Try to see the situation from her point of view. Look at his hurt and let it become your hurt. As you feel her sorrow and pain, you will begin to regret the wound you have caused.

Once you acknowledge the problem, you must go to your spouse and humbly apologize. Tell your partner specifically why you were wrong so he'll realize you take the situation seriously. Let him know you are very sorry for hurting him. Ask, "Will you forgive me?" With these words you take responsibility for your actions and submit to your spouse's mercy.

Even if you have done everything perfectly to this point, your spouse might not be ready to forgive. Some people can forgive easily and quickly, while others need more time to work through their thoughts and feelings. Be patient.

The last step in seeking forgiveness is to change your behavior. Unfortunately, actions speak louder than words. Your intentions might be great, but what your spouse wants is to be assured that she won't be hurt again. Trust is built when you and your spouse act in a trustworthy manner. To do this you must develop a plan, prepare for what might cause you to fail, keep yourself accountable to at least one person besides your spouse, and pray together for success.

As you seek forgiveness, you open the door to healing and togetherness. If you refuse to seek forgiveness, you slam the door on your spouse's feelings and block your relationship from growing.

Couples step on each other's feet many times every day. That's why we need to be quick to seek forgiveness. If you sense a wall being built between you and your spouse, find out if you have hurt or offended him. If you have, make it right.

The flip side of this coin is granting forgiveness. Refusing to forgive traps us in our pain and keeps us from healing. Without forgiveness, trust can't be regained and the relationship begins to die. But if you've been hurt, questions surround you. Here are some of these questions and their answers:

Does he deserve to be forgiven? Probably not.
Will he do it again? Maybe.
Should you forgive him? Definitely.
Why? Because it is the right thing to do.
When should you forgive him? A.S.A.P.
When should you trust him? Not until he proves himself trustworthy.

And yet the hardest question is this: How do I forgive? Start by admitting the hurt. Be honest. Don't deny the pain. That will ultimately make things worse. Don't exaggerate it either. Accurately facing your hurt prepares you to forgive.

Forgiveness is a decision. Facing your hurt helps you to know what you are forgiving. In this way, forgiveness frees you from being controlled by the pain. You forgive not to get your spouse off the hook but to help you to be healthy and to restore your relationship. Forgiveness literally means "to give something up." At the point of forgiveness, you let go of the poisons that are accompanying the hurt: anger, hatred, disgust, bitterness, fear, resentment, depression, confusion, and alienation.

Forgiveness is a decision to look forward instead of backward. By doing this, you are making four promises to yourself and to your spouse:

1. I will not dwell on this incident.
2. I will not bring up this incident again and use it against him.
3. I will not talk to others about this incident.
4. I will not allow my bitterness about this incident to hurt our relationship.

Making these promises is not easy. Sometimes you need to ask God to help you forgive. Other times you need to think of all the hurtful things you've done to others and how they have forgiven you. If you are still stuck, consider how God has forgiven you.

Now is the time to forgive your spouse and move on. Forgiveness allows for a new beginning. There are days we all need a fresh start. So:

repair your relationship
renew your love
reestablish your dream of what could be

Every house accumulates garbage. With three kids, I am amazed at how fast we can fill all the wastepaper baskets in our house. But the trash can under the sink always seems to fill up the fastest. This also seems to be the can that is most likely to smell bad. Now, in my family, it was somehow decided in the early years of marriage that the husband must take out the garbage.

But what if I refused to do this?

Or what if Tami stood in front of the kitchen sink and wouldn't allow me to remove the garbage?

Let's say this continued for a month or two. By now the can beneath the sink is sending forth an extremely unpleasant aroma throughout the house. To put it bluntly, *it stinks.* The next step is painfully obvious: Someone needs to take out the garbage.

A marriage tends to accumulate hurts and all types of garbage. Forgiveness is simply taking out the garbage. Every day you injure each other. Every day you need to take out the garbage. But some of you have let the hurts pile up for a month or two. Some of you have even let them pile up for years. Then you act surprised when things don't smell good.

If you don't seek forgiveness and grant forgiveness, your marriage will start to rot. In time it will stink. Some couples seem to think that if their marriage starts smelling bad, they need to move to another "house." But the solution is so much simpler: If you want a sweet-smelling relationship, take out the garbage.

TODAY'S TOOLS

Prayer

Dear God,

Thank you for forgiving me for all the wrong things I've thought, said, and done. Even when I did not deserve forgiveness, you gave it freely with no strings attached. I want to be more like you.

Teach me to be more sensitive to the one I love. When I hurt my spouse, help me to be quick to seek forgiveness. Give me the courage and humility to take responsibility with no excuse or justification. Break my heart as I feel the hurt I've caused. Place the perfect words in my clumsy mouth, words that might bring help and healing.

Make me realize that to hurt the one you gave me is to hurt you.

Show me how to give grace, regardless of whether or not I feel like it, and whether or not my mate deserves it. When my spouse hurts me, give me the ability to forgive quickly and completely and sincerely, just as you have forgiven me.

Build in me a forgiving heart.

Amen

Passage

You must make allowance for each other's faults and forgive the person who offends you. Remember, the Lord forgave you, so you must forgive others. COLOSSIANS 3:13

Practice

① Review the month and list three things for which you need to ask your spouse's forgiveness. These might be attitudes or words or actions. Sometime in the next week, humbly and sincerely seek forgiveness.

② Together with your spouse, set up a "statute of limitations," and agree to a certain length of time after which you can't use a past event against one another. Determine whether the term should be one year, two years, or longer.

③ Once you've forgiven your spouse for something, write these four promises on an index card and commit them to memory:

- Do not dwell on it.
- Do not bring it up.
- Do not talk to others about it.
- Do not allow it to hinder our love.

RULE ⓮
WELCOME EACH OTHER HOME

GRANDMA BLANCHE was married thirty-eight years when my grandfather passed away. Several years later, I asked her what made her marriage so good.

She smiled the way only my grandma can smile. "The secret is simple," she whispered with a twinkle in her eye. "You always make them glad they came home."

Grandma went on to explain how she'd straighten up the house and, if she had the time, bake her famous oatmeal chocolate chip cookies. Then she'd slip into a clean dress, run a brush through her hair, freshen up her makeup, dab some perfume behind each ear, and greet her man at the front door with a welcome-home kiss.

"I wanted your grandfather to want to be here rather than any other place in the world. He worked hard, so home needed to be a place he could relax. If someone doesn't feel positive about coming home, they're going to look for excuses to stay away."

Grandma Blanche was a wise woman, but unfortunately many couples have not yet learned the secret power of a warm, positive welcome home. Because of this, too many spouses find excuses to stay away: There is always more to do at work, there are friends who want to get together, there are hobbies that would be fun to do, and there are meetings that must be attended. By themselves, there is nothing wrong with any of these activities, but if they're used to avoid coming home, there is a serious problem.

What happens in the first fifteen minutes of arriving home sets the mood for the rest of the evening. If you return home to someone who is glad to see you, you are happy to be there. If you are ignored or met with a list of everything that went wrong while you were gone, you begin to wish you were somewhere else. When things are negative at home, you tend to look for a place that's more positive.

But you've also got to be realistic, because things at home can't always be smooth. Each day when I finish my time at work, I give Tami a quick call at home. Part of this is to let her know when to expect me and to see if she needs me to pick up anything on the way home. The other part is to find out how everything is going.

When I call, I listen for Tami's stress level. Some evenings, all is well. At other times, I hear a tone of voice that says, "Get home as quick as you can because the kids are driving me crazy and I'm not sure how much longer I can keep it together."

Those are the nights I know Tami needs me either to bring home dinner or to take the kids out to McDonald's or to give her a break by watching the kids while she gets out of the house.

I'm not always as sensitive to Tami when I come home as I would like to be. With all my training as a psychologist and all the years I've worked with couples, you'd think I'd have it down pat. But I don't. One day shortly after Tami had given birth to our third child, Dusty, I came home and things were not as orderly as I thought they should be. I walked into the family room, looked around, and said one of those stupid things that make everybody cringe: "What have you been doing all day?"

Immediately, as I saw the tears form in Tami's eyes and her cheeks flush, I knew I had made a big mistake. So instead of trying desperately to dig my way out of the hole I'd just fallen into, I said, "Excuse me. Let me try this all over again."

I turned around, walked out the front door, climbed into my car, and drove around the block. A few minutes later I returned and rang the doorbell. When Tami opened the door, I put my arms around her and gave her a huge kiss. "How could I be lucky enough to be married to the most beautiful girl in the whole world? I've missed you all day and I am so glad to finally be home."

That's the sort of welcome Tami deserves. Even though I blew it the first time, at least I had the wisdom to try it again and get it right the second time around.

I wish I could tell you I've learned my lesson and haven't complained about the neatness of the house since, but old habits don't die easily. One summer evening I came home and Tami was sitting on the front porch talking with one of our wonderful children. As I walked toward her, I said something like, "This yard looks like a disaster. Doesn't anybody around here know how to put anything away where it belongs?"

At that point, Tami, with all her sensitivity and insight, said the perfect thing to stop me in my tracks.

Without standing up or raising her voice, she matter-of-factly said, "I have been wondering all day what you would like me to do. I asked myself, 'Would Steve rather I keep the house and yard in perfect order, or would he rather I focus my energy on our kids?' I figured you would rather I spend my time doing what has the most long-term value." Then with a large smile she said, "So that is what I've been doing all day."

What could I say?

In a few well-crafted sentences, she'd taken the wind out of my sails. She was obviously so right that there was nothing more I could say. So I sat down beside her and watched our kids ride their bikes around our cul-de-sac.

Welcoming each other home is something that can transform your relationship, but it doesn't always come naturally. If you're at home, anticipate when your beloved will arrive and create a welcome he'll appreciate. If your spouse likes order, try to give order; if she comes home hungry, have something ready; if he likes peace and quiet, find a calm room for him to relax in; if she loves to be hugged and kissed, embrace her. Tailor your welcome to what your spouse enjoys most.

On the other hand, if you are the one returning home, use your travel time to get into a positive attitude. On the way home, relax and consider all you have to be thankful for. When you get there, leave the stresses and frustrations at the front door. Think of compliments you'd like to say and fun things you'd like to do. Psych yourself up so that you are excited to be home. When you step through the door, let your spouse know you are glad to finally be where you really belong.

There are two major problems that I hear from couples with regard to coming home. Both of these tendencies can destroy your sense of togetherness.

First, there is the exhaustion factor. After a hard day spent on the job, running errands, or caring for the kids, a couple gets worn out. Too often a husband and wife spend all their energy during the day, and they give each other only what's left over. At the end of the day all they have is exhaustion: tired meals, tired fun, tired talk, and even tired sex. The solution is to pace themselves and save some energy for a quality evening.

Second, there is the isolation factor. This is a tendency that strikes more men than women. We get home after a long day and we want a break from people. So we pull away from our beloved to read the newspaper, watch the television, play with the computer, or whatever solitary activity we enjoy most. The only way to overcome isolation is to commit to spending more time together. Don't let hobbies, special interests, or relaxation take priority over the person God has given you.

If every person welcomed his spouse home with loving enthusiasm, you'd be surprised at the positive impact it would have on marriages. Suddenly couples would yearn to spend more time together, and home would truly become a place of joy, comfort, and peace.

TODAY'S TOOLS

Prayer

Dear God,

Forgive me for those days that I get so wrapped up in my own agenda that I don't actively, lovingly welcome my spouse home. Help me to make my partner's homecoming the highlight of his day.

Also forgive me for coming home stressed or critical. Plant in my heart the desire to come home with a great attitude to love my spouse unconditionally.

Teach me how to make our home a haven of joy, peace, and faith. Show me how to create a safe harbor and refuge that is close to your heart—a place where the storms of life will not damage our love.

Direct me in ways that will make each homecoming special and all that follows it positive, encouraging, and delightful.

Make me a blessing to my spouse.

Amen

Passage

Greet each other in Christian love. 1 PETER 5:14

Practice

① The next time you're headed home, prepare your heart by doing at least two of the following:

- Slow down.
- Clear out the negative thoughts.
- Think about positive things.
- Thank God for your spouse.
- Plan one way to show your love when you get home.
- Consider what your partner needs most from you.
- Rehearse joyful memories.
- Practice compliments.
- Pray for your attitude.
- Relax.

② The next time your spouse arrives home, greet her with a hug and a kiss.

③ Discuss with your partner how the "exhaustion factor" and the "isolation factor" might be impacting your marriage. Develop a plan that allows you to resolve each of these problems at least one night per week.

RULE ⓯
GO TO BED AT THE SAME TIME

"I'M A NIGHT PERSON," Daniel explained to me. "I love staying up as late as I can. Sometimes I watch TV, sometimes I read a good book, but whatever I do, I don't go to bed before 1 A.M."

"Linda is my opposite," Daniel continued. "She is the classic morning person. She is up at 5:30 every morning. But to be alive that early, she has to be in bed by 10:00. Therefore we have different sleep schedules, and we rarely go to bed at the same time."

"How do you feel about that?" I asked him.

"It doesn't bother me," he said, "but Linda hates it."

"Why?"

"She says it makes her feel lonely, angry, and disconnected."

I'm amazed at how many couples go to bed at different times. Maybe it's normal, but it's not necessarily healthy for a vital marriage.

Too many couples live parallel lives. They spend much of their time doing different jobs, enjoying different hobbies, and talking with different friends. If a couple isn't careful, this creates a distant marriage. Sure, partners might eat together, go to church together, and even sleep in the same bed, but they've lost their sense of closeness.

When you go to bed at the same time, you create a perfect opportunity to reconnect and rebuild your togetherness. To end the day together is a reminder that the two of you are one. So set aside some quality time just before you go to sleep. Make this a special time. Go into your bedroom together and close the door, shutting out all the busyness, stress, and distractions of the world.

Sheila and David go to their bedroom every night around 9:30. Sheila set up two chairs and a small table in a corner of their bedroom. Here they share a bowl of ice cream and review their day together. Sheila told me that setting up this time saved their marriage. Before they began this tradition, she would go to sleep alone each night while David stayed up late. As Sheila lay in bed by herself, she grew lonely, critical, and negative. She felt rejected and began to think her husband didn't really care about her anymore. Each night she fell asleep with thoughts and feelings of how distant she was from David.

The last thing on your mind as you go to sleep is processed by your brain all night long. If you are unhappy or angry with your spouse as you lay in bed, there is a good chance that you'll continue those thoughts in your sleep world. Your brain never shuts down; throughout the night it's just as active as during the day. So if you go to sleep with positive feelings toward your spouse, those feelings get repeated and deeply embedded. Then when you awake, you'll still feel great about your mate. But if you go to sleep angry or disconnected, that's how you will awake. Since you spend one-fourth to one-third of your married life asleep, it's important that you go to sleep with positive thoughts.

Going to bed with a positive attitude toward each other sometimes takes work. The apostle Paul wrote, "Do not let the sun go down while you are still angry" (Ephesians 4:26, NIV). My paraphrase of this is, "Don't argue in bed! Resolve your issues, or at least let go of them, before it gets too late at night." Many couples save their arguments for their bedroom, but I would encourage you to keep them out of the bedroom. This ought to be the most positive room in your house. Make it a pleasant place of peace to which you and your spouse long to escape. Clear out the clutter, give it a fresh coat of paint, set up a CD player, add some romantic touches, and create an atmosphere that you both enjoy. If your bedroom is a positive place to be, you'll be drawn to it more often.

The half hour before bedtime can be the best time of your day. If you're creative with this special time, it will build wonderful memories, intimate moments, and a better marriage. George and Mattie have figured out an innovative method to make the end of each day something they truly look forward to. On each evening of the week they do a different activity just before they go to bed:

Monday nights: Get out the massage oil and give each other back rubs.

Tuesday nights: Crawl onto the bed and read a novel to each other.

Wednesday nights: Come up with three questions to ask each other.

Thursday nights: Watch a favorite video or TV show together while cuddled up on the bed or the couch.

Friday nights: Go on a date and come home to talk about positive memories you've had with each other.

Saturday nights: Share your favorite dessert and talk about your dreams of a future together.

Sunday nights: Do a devotional together from a book such as *My Utmost for His Highest* (by Oswald Chambers) or *Night Light* (by James and Shirley Dobson).

Each of these activities has become a weekly tradition for George and Mattie. And when they finish the activity, George and Mattie make sure to give each other a hug and a kiss. Sometimes it leads to something more.

By going into the bedroom and getting into bed together, you can create a time for sharing with one another. Lying side by side, looking into one another's eyes, make a real effort to share what's on your heart. At the end of the day, your defenses are down and this allows your heart to be more open.

Many people feel that the half hour before bed is the best time of the whole day. But if you don't go to bed at the same time, you'll miss this opportunity. This is much more than an opportunity to share; it's an opportunity to make your marriage better.

We could all benefit from a better marriage.

TODAY'S TOOLS

Prayer

Dear God,

Protect my evening time, when the sun goes down and the world grows quiet. Allow this to be a time that draws my beloved and me closer together. May this be the best part of our day—a time we anticipate, protect, and treasure.

Teach me how to make our time at night positive: listening, loving, and sharing with each other.

When the day is gone, remind me to reach out to my spouse. Motivate me to make our bedroom a place that draws us in, so we can truly connect, appreciate each other, and grow deeper in love.

Forgive me for the times I have selfishly not made our going to bed together a priority. Also forgive me for the nights I have allowed my spouse to go to sleep alone, lonely, or angry.

Thank you for giving me that special someone with whom I can share my bedtime.

Amen

Passage

And on a cold night, two under the same blanket can gain warmth from each other. But how can one be warm alone? ECCLESIASTES 4:11

Practice

① If one of you prefers to go to bed early and the other prefers to go to bed late, discuss how you might find a middle ground where you can connect before you fade into sleep.

② Develop three different end-of-the-day connecting ideas. During the next week try each of them, evaluating which ones you would most like to try again.

③ Set aside an evening where you slip into bed early. Light candles and enjoy a special dessert while you share stories, memories, ideas, opinions, questions, dreams, encouragements, and anything that can make you both smile.

④ Promise each other that you will never go to sleep angry at each other and that you will always go to sleep with a kiss, a hug, a prayer, or an "I love you."

RULE **16**
DEVELOP MUTUAL FRIENDS

"I WANT SOME EXCITEMENT," said Matt. "Tina's just no fun anymore."

"If you would help more with the kids, maybe she'd have the energy to have more fun," said Jim, one of Matt's best friends.

"I know Tina's a good woman and I love her, but I'm just not *in love* with her anymore."

"Love is a choice and a commitment," said Lori, Jim's wife. "If you work on being a more loving husband, then you might be able to recapture those feelings."

"But you don't understand," said Matt. "I've found someone else. It wouldn't be fair to stay with Tina and pretend I'm in love with her when I've given my heart to someone else."

"What effect do you think this will have on the children?" asked Jim.

"I don't know."

"Don't you think you should talk to the pastor or a marriage counselor or somebody?" said Lori.

Jim and Lori continued their conversation with Matt until he finally agreed to meet with their pastor and discuss the state of his marriage. During the next few months, Matt and Tina spent a lot of time with their good friends Jim and Lori, who helped them through this crisis. A year later, Matt and Tina renewed their marriage vows with special thanks to their good friends.

Every couple needs good mutual friends. Years ago, before our culture became so mobile, most married couples lived close to their parents, grandparents, uncles, aunts, and cousins. Many stayed in the same community all their lives and few moved away from strong families and lifelong friends. That was a time when people grew up knowing the names of their neighbors and building close relationships with those around them. Because of this, there was a built-in support system. These days, we've become so independent and busy that we're disconnected from family and community. Therefore, mutual friends are more important than ever before in helping a marriage to succeed.

Friends can help you through the rough times in a marriage, and they can enrich the positive times in your relationship. Friends can make a good marriage better, supporting and protecting all that is important.

On the flip side, friends who aren't emotionally healthy or stable can create a lot of tension and frustration in a relationship and sometimes can even tear it apart. There are five aspects to friendship that can create stress and potential destruction in your marriage:

Lack of friends: If you don't have any friends, you have no support system for your relationship. This means that you'll be looking to your spouse to meet all your social, interactive, and emotional needs. No partner can meet every need. For example, many women have higher communication needs, while men often have greater competition needs. Therefore, women frequently gather to communicate, and men often gather to compete. Having friends often takes some of the pressure of differing needs off the marriage.

Separate friends: Often a husband will have his male friends and a wife will have her female friends. This is healthy and normal in most situations. However, if you start spending more time with your friends than you do with your spouse or if you find yourself enjoying certain friends more than you do your spouse, you're headed for trouble. Separate friends can be good unless they create a wedge in your togetherness with your spouse. If your friends become your spouse's friends, there is less potential for division.

Negative friends: We're all influenced by our friends. When that influence is positive, everybody is happy. But if your friends speak poorly of marriage or have negative qualities that might weaken or threaten your marriage, you need to avoid them regardless of how wonderful they are. You also need to beware of friends who don't like, respect, or approve of your spouse. Even if these friends are right, such attitudes need to be handled in a considerate, constructive way. If your friends are rude to your spouse, minimize contact with them. Lastly, friends who have a more relative value system than you have can easily lead you in a direction you will someday regret.

Opposite-sex friends: Maybe you relate better to members of the opposite sex, and maybe your closest friends are of the opposite sex, but these relationships pose a potential danger to your marriage. They can trigger jealousies, and you run the risk of becoming more intimate than either of you may have intended. Be careful about spending too much time alone with those of the opposite sex, especially sharing deep emotions and difficulties or doing fun and recreational activities together. Even though a situation may be perfectly innocent, it can have a questionable appearance. Besides, innocent situations can easily escalate into not-so-innocent situations. Don't be naïve.

Too many friends: Some people are so social and extroverted that they fill their lives with as many friends as possible. While these friends may be positive and healthy, too many of them can create problems. Too many friends will start to consume more and more of your time, along with more and more of your energy. And soon, you'll have less time and energy for your marriage. Remember, your spouse is your primary companion; don't let anything undermine this relationship. Too much of a good thing is not healthy. That's true of chocolate, sports, and even friends.

Healthy friendships take a lot of pressure off a marriage and strengthen it in ways that are invaluable. Friends provide a place to vent frustrations, check out perceptions, talk about things our partner has no interest in, and participate in activities our spouse doesn't care about.

Finding another couple with whom to spend time has many benefits you may never have thought about. Yet in choosing another couple it's important that you both feel comfortable with the choice. Often two wives will connect and enjoy their time together so much that they assume their husbands will naturally become good friends. Sometimes such a friendship develops, but sometimes it doesn't. Be sensitive to the fact that some personalities don't click, regardless of how hard you push and pray. Once you find another couple with whom you both click, you will realize what a treasure you have found.

Here are some of the many benefits of having healthy, mutual couple friends:

They remind you of what's normal in a relationship.
They encourage habits, activities, and attitudes that build a good marriage.
They provide a place to vent and work through everyday marital frustrations.
They confront wrong, foolish, illegal, and insensitive behavior.
They offer opportunities for fun social interaction.

They bring new ideas for strengthening, improving, and revitalizing your marriage.

Mutual friends can also encourage you to make it through the rough times. When Ben and Rachael lost most of their earthly possessions in a horrible house fire, stress, anger, and depression quickly overwhelmed them.

"How could this happen?"

"Why would God allow this?"

"What should we do now?"

When Ben discovered that their home insurance had lapsed because Rachael had not been paying the premiums, and nothing was covered, everything grew worse.

"How could you do this to us? What were you thinking? Don't you realize that because of you, we have now lost everything?"

Yet Ben and Rachael had developed friendships with many couples from church. These mutual friends put together a number of major fund-raisers to gather enough money for Ben and Rachael to rebuild their home. One couple invited them to move into their house for more than a year without paying a cent. Another couple donated all the lumber for the new house. Many other couples worked evenings and weekends doing everything from plumbing to putting up walls to laying tile. Fifteen months later, Ben and Rachael moved into their new home with mortgage payments less than they had been paying prior to the fire.

Ben told me that without mutual friends, their marriage would never have survived the fire. But now he has a new house and is more in love with his wife than ever before. If you ask Ben, "What is the most significant lesson you have learned through all of this?" he will smile and say, "Thank God for friends."

TODAY'S TOOLS

Prayer

Dear God,

Thank you for the good friends you have given us. And thank you that you have been the best friend of all.

Bring into our marriage healthy, positive, mutual friends. Help us to appreciate those friends and give back to them the good gifts they have given to us.

Provide me with the courage and wisdom to say no to friends who might damage or undermine our marriage. Create in me a bold and faithful heart that will not hesitate to protect our marriage from risky relationships, even if those friends are nice, attractive, sensitive, exciting, or fun.

Show me how to be a good friend to my spouse. Build in me the qualities that might encourage and enrich the marriages of the couples we meet.

Make us good examples of what you would like a marriage to be. And bring us alongside couples in trouble that might need another couple that cares.

Amen

Passage

A friend is always loyal. PROVERBS 17:17

Practice

① Sit down with your spouse and talk about the friends you each have. Look at the five aspects of friendship that can create stress and ask your spouse if any of your current friendships fit into these categories. Together, explore options of how you can overcome this challenge.

② Make a list of couples that could be healthy, supportive, and mature friends. Ask one of these couples over to your house sometime during the next week.

③ Consider the couples you know who are having trouble or have been married a shorter time than you. Commit to joining with your spouse and encouraging one of these couples in creative, positive ways every week for the next six months.

RULE ⑰
TAKE A DATE

"LET'S GO ON A PICNIC DINNER."

"Where?" I asked.

"At this great park where they have evening concerts," Tami said. "We can get some food at this new restaurant and enjoy the music at the park."

Tami made arrangements for our kids and off we went. We enjoyed the picnic dinner as we watched the sun set to the beat of old-time fifties rock and roll.

"What do you want to do next?" Tami asked.

"There was that romantic movie you wanted to see," I said.

Tami was delighted as we drove to a theater and had a great time together. After the movie we shared an incredibly rich and wonderful dessert at an elegant downtown restaurant. As we closed the evening, Tami wanted to catch a view of the city lights from the top of a nearby hotel. As we went up the elevator, Tami pressed the wrong button.

Then she reached into her purse, pulled out a hotel room key, and said, "Our kids are spending the night with friends."

I was shocked.

The hotel room was filled with candlelight and love songs. That afternoon Tami had packed an overnight bag for both of us and delivered it to the room. She had decorated everything and even scattered rose petals over the bed.

The next morning we slept in, read novels, shared mochas and sweet rolls, and explored downtown Portland. What a fantastic date!

Every time I think about that date, I am reminded of my love for Tami. Dating is a way to express your appreciation, create romance, show respect, add significance, and share love. If you don't date your mate, you risk sending the opposite message:

> You don't appreciate him.
> You don't care about romance.
> You don't respect her.
> You don't see him as significant.
> Maybe you don't even love her anymore.

Couples don't usually decide to stop dating; it just happens. Sometimes the responsibilities of work or family take all your time. Sometimes the hectic pace of life takes all your energy, leaving you too tired and exhausted for much else. Other times you just get lazy and fall into a rut of inactivity and distraction. Then there are the two big logistical problems: no money and no child care. But if you want a great marriage, you won't use any of these excuses, for love always finds a way.

How can something that once was so easy become so hard? It doesn't have to be! All you have to do is remember a few simple principles:

Schedule it. If you don't schedule dates, you won't have dates. Pull out your calendar and mark down your dates for the next several months. Sometimes it's easier to circle a particular evening each week and make this your regular date night. I know a couple that makes every Monday their movie-date night. But it doesn't have to be in the evening to be a date. If it's more convenient, schedule breakfast dates or midday dates. It's not important when they happen; it's just important that they happen.

It's amazing how expensive dating can get if you aren't careful. So make sure you write weekly dates into your budget. Set aside money that can only be used for going out together. Don't think of this as wasted or frivolous money; it's an investment in your marriage. And if you don't make regular investments, you might find your relationship going bankrupt. But if finances are tight, this doesn't mean you can't date. There are thousands of things you can do for little or no money. You can go for a drive, fly a kite, walk through a garden, play tennis, or even people-watch. One couple I know often goes for a coffee date at a local bookstore. Another couple enjoys a window-shopping date at a nearby mall.

Trade it. What should you do and who should plan it? This is where some couples get stuck. Others get frustrated because one partner ends up doing all the work of arranging the dates. This sometimes leaves the impression that the other partner doesn't care about dating or isn't willing to put forth much effort. To solve this problem I encourage couples to trade off. The husband plans and makes all the arrangements for one date. This includes deciding on the activity, arranging for child care, and planning the meals. The wife plans and arranges the next date. Then you repeat the process. When your partner is in charge of the date, cooperate and be positive even if what he chooses to do isn't your favorite thing. The next week you'll be in charge.

Energize it. When you date, don't get stuck in a rut. If you always go to the same restaurant, it soon loses its special appeal. The best dates hold at least some uniqueness, wonder, variety, or creativity. So try new things. Maybe you'll develop a new favorite. And if you don't, at least you've created a new memory. Doing things that are new or different energizes your dating and keeps your love alive. Boredom can kill your spirit and your relationship. So energize it.

Communicate it. The most important thing about your dates is not what you do or where you go but how you communicate. Talking and listening—just the two of you, without distraction—can be one of the most positive times of your week. So whatever you do, make sure intimate, honest, deep-down communication is a part of it. When you know one another intimately, your marriage becomes more emotionally rewarding than ever. Share your heart and discover the heart of your mate. Get close, but avoid talking about schedules, money, children, or complaints. Save those talks for another time. Keep your date talk focused on learning more about one another's heart.

Romance it. Romance is not optional. If you ignore it, your dates will suffer and ultimately your marriage will suffer. Too many couples let romance slip away because it's not easy. But easy or not, it is important. Romance involves the old-fashioned word *chivalry*. The word may be old-fashioned, but the concept isn't. Chivalry can be a knight in shining armor rescuing his beloved. It can be a gentleman laying his coat across the mud so his lady won't get her shoes dirty. It can be a husband opening his wife's car door. However it looks, chivalry is courtesy and kindness and letting your spouse know you treasure him. Romance also involves generosity and selflessness. Romance can make the simplest date a smashing success.

Enjoy it. When you go on a date, do everything you can to please your partner and make it a great experience. Know what she likes and where she likes to go. Do it his way. I get the most joy from seeing Tami relaxed and having a wonderful time. I want to give her my attention, my heart, and my best attitude. So have fun, smile, laugh, and do the things the two of you enjoy most. Make your time together the best. Fill it with joy and closeness—

emotional, intellectual, and physical. Show your spouse what love is all about.

Apply these principles to whatever type of date you have, and you will never regret it.

Here are the four major types of dating:

Traditional dates involve dinners or movies or drives in the country. They may be expensive or may not cost a penny; they may be active or may be laid-back. They are wonderful, and they are within the realm of normal.

Extreme dates are highly unusual and beyond the norm. A friend of mine is a flight attendant who surprised his wife with breakfast in Paris. Now *that* was an extreme date! You, too, may have experienced certain highly special dates that you'll never forget. If these happen once a year, you should be happy. If they don't, plan one.

In-house dates happen when finances, child care, or exhaustion limit your freedom. In-house dates should never become a replacement for traditional dates, but they can periodically provide another option. There are plenty of enjoyable activities right at home: a candlelit dinner, watching a DVD or video together, or snuggling up on the sofa as you listen to your most romantic CD.

Lastly, **social dates** are when another couple joins you. Sometimes it's fun and can even add variety if you invite a few other people to join your date. Like in-house dates, these should be the exception rather than the rule. Also, you must be careful to choose others who are positive and healthy—and whom you both enjoy.

Dating brought you together with your partner, and it can keep you together. Dating pulls you above the ordinary, allowing you special time to communicate and connect. Enjoying some type of date on a weekly basis will improve your marriage and help you to appreciate each other even more.

TODAY'S TOOLS

Prayer

Dear God,

Encourage me to date my spouse more often—really date like before we were married. Place this desire deep in my heart and help me turn it into reality.

Forgive me for the times I have not treated my beloved as kindly and specially as she deserves. Forgive me for the excuses I have given for not going out on regular dates.

Show me how to date in a generous and selfless way, always demonstrating by attitude, action, and word how special my mate truly is to me.

Teach me how to date with so much chivalry that it overflows into every aspect of my marriage. Give me a renewed feeling of romance in my heart and let it shine on my spouse even when I'm not in the best mood.

Help us remember you in all that we do. Bring us closer to each other and to you with every date. Thank you for being the source of love.

Amen

Passage

Young man: "Yes, compared to other women, my beloved is like a lily among thorns."

Young woman: "And compared to other youths, my lover is like the finest apple tree in the orchard. I am seated in his delightful shade, and his fruit is delicious to eat. He brings me to the banquet hall, so everyone can see how much he loves me." Song of Songs 2:2-4

Practice

① Ask your spouse out on a date to do something you know he would enjoy, even if it isn't your first preference. Take him to his favorite restaurant or go see a movie he's wanted to see. Do all you can to make it a special and memorable time for him.

② Sit down together and schedule two dates for the upcoming month. Talk about how you can make this happen in terms of money, child care, planning, interests, and any other details that might sabotage your dates.

③ Visit a local coffee shop together and share your memories of the best dates you've ever had with each other.

RULE ⓲
MAKE LOVE

HOW CAN SOMETHING that is so incredible for some couples be so difficult for others?

Sexuality is one of the most private and sensitive aspects of a marriage. For some couples it is wonderful, for others it's overstated, and for still others it's a curse. I have been surprised to discover that 75 percent of the couples that seek my help struggle with some aspect of their sexual relationship.

"I hate sex!" said Candy.

"But I love you," said Tony. "Have I done anything that turns you off?"

"No, you're a great husband," she said. "It's just hard for me to enjoy sex."

Candy had been sexually abused as a child, and as a single adult many of those she dated did not respect her sexual boundaries. Tony had been one of the exceptions; he had always treated her respectfully and they had not made love until their wedding night. Yet during the first year of their marriage, Candy and Tony had made love only five times. During the next two years it had decreased to nothing.

"Don't you love me anymore?" Tony asked.

"Of course I do," she said. "Is sex the only way to prove it to you? Does everything have to come down to sex?"

"No! But if you really loved me, you'd want to be with me physically."

"I do want to be with you, but it's not that easy. And the fact that you are pressuring me makes it even harder. It feels like all men ever want is sex. I need to know you love me for who I am, not because of my body."

"Candy, we've been married for three years. Look at all we've done together. You've got to know I love you for who you are."

"Then why can't we just ignore the sexual stuff for a while? I'll work on it and when I'm ready we can make love, and then everything will be all right."

"I've been extremely patient," said Tony. "I can't go on like this much longer. I'm a healthy male, and I've shut down my sexual side for over two years. This is not right. It's not fair. This is not what marriage is supposed to be like. If you don't want me, maybe somebody else will."

Tony stomped out of the apartment, slamming the door behind him. Candy collapsed in tears.

Men and women are wired differently; this is especially true in the sexual arena. For many men, physical intimacy opens the heart to emotional intimacy. For women the opposite is usually true—emotional intimacy opens the heart to physical intimacy. Therefore, if there has just been a conflict, a man might want a sexual connection. That is his way of resolving everything. For a woman, sex may be the last thing on her mind. She needs to feel peace with her husband before she has any desire to make love with him.

Another common difference involves arousal. Men can usually be aroused and feel amorous very quickly, regardless of the time and setting. Women often build toward amorous feelings and are aroused slowly, with time and setting significantly related to the process. Men tend to operate like a light switch: they are either turned off or turned on. Women tend to operate more like a dimmer switch: they slowly turn the light up. Gary Smalley, an expert on relationships, has joined me several times on my radio show. On one of those visits, he used a different metaphor, saying men are like microwave ovens and women are like Crock-Pots.

A third difference involves stress. For a woman to feel arousal, she usually needs to relax. In fact, for many women the greater the relaxation, the greater the arousal. They need to be able to clear their minds, relax their bodies, and focus positively on the one they love. Any potential distraction (such as children, strange noises, physical discomfort, self-consciousness, or anxiety) can kill the mood and steal their arousal. For a man, stress often increases his arousal. The greater the stress, the more desire he feels and the more intense his drive for sexual release. A man may become so focused at this point that he doesn't even notice those things that distract his wife. Only after climax does he relax, and then he often falls asleep. Women, on the other hand, frequently find they feel energized after lovemaking.

Because of all couples' inevitable differences, sexual communication is very important. Yet most couples rarely talk about their physical relationship—their needs, expectations, preferences, fears, comfort zones, and sensitivities. With a little communication, a couple can avoid a lot of confusion, hurt, and misunderstanding. Talking brings you closer, and though it might not solve all your sexual struggles, it at least allows you to understand them better. As you talk, remember that healthy lovemaking is not selfish or greedy. It is patient. It is caring. It is neither pushy nor demanding. It always puts the needs and sensitivities of your partner above your own.

Sexuality involves "the three G's." First, sex is **good.** "God saw all that he had made, and it was very good" (Genesis 1:31, NIV). God created sex, and when it is expressed unselfishly within the boundaries of marriage, it is a mutual blessing.

Sex is **glue.** "For this reason a man will leave his father and mother and be united to his wife, and they will become one flesh" (Genesis 2:24, NIV). Sexuality protects a couple from outside temptations and bonds them closer together than any other relationship can.

Sex is a **gift.** "The wife's body does not belong to her alone but also to her husband. In the same way, the husband's body does not belong to him alone but also to his wife" (1 Corinthians 7:4, NIV). Freely giving yourself to your spouse with no expectations in return is true romance.

Keeping "the three G's" in mind, all couples should make it a priority to make love at least once a week. Try not to make love simply out of desire, habit, or duty. Make love in a way that shows love. To do this, every couple must look at the big picture. Lovemaking is a lot more than a few minutes of physical intimacy; it should be a well-thought-out event.

Lovemaking consists of at least six very important components. If you want a positive sexual connection with your spouse, pay attention to each of these components:

1. **Context:** A couple's interaction in the twelve hours before lovemaking sets the context for closeness. Be kind and caring. Pay attention to each other. Remember that sincere, meaningful lovemaking grows from a context of love.

2. **Atmosphere:** Draw each other into romance by creating an atmosphere that feeds all five senses. Here are a few suggestions:
   Hearing: romantic music
   Sight: candlelight, flowers
   Touch: bubble bath, satin sheets, massage oil
   Taste: chocolate, fruit, sparkling cider
   Smell: scented candles, special perfume/cologne

3. **Connection:** Someone once said that women spell sex "T-A-L-K." This has more truth than many men realize. Talking can warm your wife and help her to be more open to you. When a guy shares his heart, listens, shows thoughtfulness, touches and caresses his

wife in nonsexual ways, and helps her to relax, then she feels connected.

4. **Foreplay:** This is where a couple crosses the line from emotional intimacy to physical intimacy. Set aside at least ten to fifteen minutes for foreplay. Some women say that this component of lovemaking is the most satisfying. Learn how to give a massage that truly relaxes and brings you in sync with each other. Does your spouse enjoy back, leg, or foot rubs? Do what brings the most pleasure. Then move to cuddling and kissing. Husbands, take your time and don't rush it. Wives, if he moves too fast, don't get frustrated. He's just more aroused than you are. Calmly and gently redirect him.

5. **Interplay:** Here is where arousal reaches its climax. Allow yourself to become one with each other. Sexual togetherness is sacred and brings a couple vulnerably close to one another. It is a symbol of unity and commitment. Treasure it and keep it pure. Focus on bringing pleasure and fulfillment to your partner. Remember that love is patient and places your beloved before yourself.

6. **Follow-through:** Never allow lovemaking to end abruptly or negatively. A bad ending can ruin a great book or an excellent movie. This is equally true with your most intimate times. After your sexual time, lie in each other's arms. Talk for a moment or two, complimenting and thanking your spouse for sharing her body. Then create closure on this most precious time with a gentle kiss or a prayer—or even both.

Sexuality should bring a couple closer, but all too often it does the opposite. If it has been a while since you've made love, something is probably wrong that you need to work out. I realize there are times of exhaustion, health difficulties, or separation that might create a period of abstinence. But this should be the exception, not the rule. If there is any difficulty in this area, don't ignore it. Talk to a physician, psychologist, counselor, or pastor. Remember, making love is an important way to show your love. And as you show your love, your marriage will grow stronger, deeper, and more exciting.

TODAY'S TOOLS

Prayer

Dear God,

Help me to understand the needs, expectations, preferences, fears, comfort zones, and sensitivities of the one I love. Then teach the two of us to talk about this aspect of our life in a way that brings us closer together.

When frustrations arise in our lovemaking, show us how to be patient and understanding toward each other.

Thank you for creating sex as a symbol of our marriage. Thank you for making sex good. Help us to keep it that way. Thank you for making sex glue. Help it to keep us close for the rest of our lives. Thank you for making sex a gift. Help us to give it with meaning, generosity, and selflessness.

Forgive me for the times I have placed sexual pleasure above love, stimulation above sensitivity, and my needs above my spouse's.

Show me how I might be the best sexual partner possible to my spouse.

Amen

Passage

The husband should not deprive his wife of sexual intimacy, which is her right as a married woman, nor should the wife deprive her husband. 1 Corinthians 7:3

Practice

① Sit down together and talk honestly about "the three G's." Discuss how gender differences and personality differences may affect your love life. Then agree on a level of sexual frequency and an approach with which you both feel comfortable.

② Do all you can to assure a positive context and an emotional connection before you initiate sexual times. Try giving a heartfelt compliment, making a romantic phone call, surprising her with her favorite coffee drink or dessert, showing an extra portion of kindness, or simply doing whatever you can to make the day positive for your spouse.

③ The next time you consider a sexual connection, set up a romantic atmosphere that includes at least four of the five senses.

④ Commit to at least ten to fifteen minutes of foreplay before making love. During this time, cuddle, kiss, relax, and communicate to your spouse how much you love him.

RULE ⓳
PRAY FOR YOUR SPOUSE

LINDA WAS TIRED. She had done everything she could think of to get her husband to change, but he wouldn't budge an inch. She asked, begged, bribed, threatened, and humiliated him. His only response was to get angry and even more stuck in his bad habits.

Finally one night in desperate frustration she cried out, "God, I don't know what to do."

That's when it happened.

Linda heard a soft voice, more like a whisper, say, "Why don't you pray?"

She looked around, but no one was there.

Speaking more to herself than to the invisible whisperer, she said, "What was that?"

"Why don't you pray?" came the voice.

Linda believed in prayer. She prayed for her children and for her finances, and she prayed that life would go smoothly. She used to pray for John, but that was years ago. Now that he was a jerk, she felt he didn't deserve her prayers.

But what about the voice? Maybe I should pray for him. After all, he is my husband and the father of my children. Besides, it couldn't hurt.

So Linda bowed her head and prayed, "God, please soften his heart, change his attitude, and better his behavior."

But these were empty words. She had given up hope years ago, and she didn't believe for a moment that anything would wake John from his neglect and abuse.

The next day she prayed for John again. It seemed stupid and fruitless, and she had no idea why she wasted her time. Yet it seemed like the right thing to do, and John had always said she was "a sucker for doing the right thing."

Every day for a week Linda prayed for her husband, and each day it became a little easier. The bitterness in her voice began to fade, her impatience lessened, and all John's irritating habits seemed easier to overlook. With all her prayers, John was no different—he was just as rude and crude as always. But what surprised her was that *she* was different. With each prayer, *her* heart softened, *her* attitude changed, and *her* behavior became better. What was meant for John had impacted her instead. In the process, a peace overtook her spirit, pushing aside some of her anger, hatred, and bitterness.

At the end of the week, even John noticed the difference. "Linda," he said awkwardly, placing his hand on hers. "Would you like to go out to dinner?"

Linda was shocked. *What's the catch? This has to be a trick. What's he after?*

"How about Chinese food?" she said.

"That sounds great," he said.

Something's wrong. He sounds nice. He sounds safe. This is too good to be true.

Over the next six months, Linda continued to pray for John. During this time she let go of her anger and drew closer to him. John stopped being so abusive and started taking Linda out on dates. Things weren't perfect, but they were so much better than before.

A pastor once said that prayer is the first step to meeting any challenge. Linda is glad she prayed. She's excited her prayers were answered. But what truly amazes her is that these prayers made *her* different. And as she changed, so did John.

I believe that we all have a responsibility to pray for our spouses daily. Don't just pray when you are feeling loving, happy, or appreciative. Pray when you are:

lonely, empty, or broken
frustrated, fighting, or angry
disgusted, disappointed, or disconnected

A friend of mine once said that prayer should be the key that opens each morning and the bolt that locks up each night. If every spouse prayed sincerely for his partner each morning and evening, marriages would be much healthier. But often it's not the person who's being prayed for who changes the most, it's the person who prays.

There are at least ten things that anyone who is married should pray about:

Yourself: Pray that you will be the best spouse you can be. Ask forgiveness for those times you have been selfish or insensitive. Focus on loving your partner more, always treating him with courtesy and compassion. Pray that you will change your negative or neglectful attitude. As we improve our words and behavior, we pave the way for our spouse to make similar changes.

Your marriage: Pray that the two of you will find a oneness that will bring you closer together. Too often couples drift apart from each other and lose that special sense of love and joy that was present at the beginning. Pray that you both will make your marriage a priority, committing time to understanding each other and placing your spouse's needs above your own.

Safety: September 11, 2001, will not be soon forgotten. How many husbands and wives kissed each other good-bye for the last time that morning?

No one knows for sure what danger lies around the next corner. Pray for your spouse's safety and protection in a world that is more dangerous than any of us wish to admit.

Health: Many of us try to eat healthy, exercise regularly, take vitamins daily, and visit a doctor when needed. These are good things, but prayer has more potential power than all four of these combined. Pray for your partner's health and strength. Pray that her body would be able to fight minor illnesses and major diseases and that her life would be long and free from sickness.

Stress: Life is full of pressure and expectations. We race from one point to another, trying to force more into a day than is reasonable. This stress frequently steals our peace and enjoyment. It makes us irritable and impatient. It opens doors to worry, depression, burnout, and all sorts of physical symptoms. Pray that your spouse will not be overwhelmed by the stress of life. Pray that he will be able to relax and find contentment in all he does.

Temptations: We all have times when we're tempted to do things that are not good for us or our marriage. Some people face such strong temptations that they have what are called *addictive personalities*. Others have less potent but equally dangerous temptations. Given the right situation, any of us could fall into temptation. Know your partner's weaknesses and struggles— whether it's alcohol, food, pornography, overspending, drugs, gambling, or anything else. Then pray for your partner.

Work: Some partners struggle with laziness and others struggle with workaholism. Neither extreme is healthy. Pray that your partner will find a balance in his work. Pray that it will bring him a sense of fulfillment. Our jobs, whether they're inside or outside the home, impact how we feel about ourselves and our marriages. Pray that your partner's job will be a positive part of his life, filling him with a sense of meaning, purpose, and personal satisfaction.

Fears: We all have fears. These fears can be overwhelming and maybe even irrational. Know your partner's fears. Do they have to do with safety, finances, failure, or death? Pray that these fears will not paralyze your spouse but that she can work through them and overcome them. Also, pray that you can be patient and understanding, doing all that you can to help and bring comfort. Never ridicule or belittle your spouse for her fears. Be a source of reassurance and support.

Dreams: Every couple and all individuals need to have dreams. Without dreams, people grow discouraged, and life becomes empty or meaningless. Dreams add focus, excitement, joy, and hope. But dreams can easily be killed or deflated. Share your dreams with each other and pray that your partner's dreams will come true. Encourage him and cheer him on. If he doesn't have a dream, help him to develop one. If he's given up on a dream, see if it can be resurrected. If you know his dreams, pray like crazy that they'll be fulfilled.

Faith: As you pray for your partner's faith, you are, in fact, praying for all of the previous nine areas. Faith impacts every aspect of one's life. If your partner struggles with her faith, don't preach or pressure. Instead, pray and live an example of a godly life. I have heard hundreds of stories of how a spouse's persistent prayers opened the heart of a partner.

Alfred Lord Tennyson once said, "More things are wrought by prayer than this world dreams of." Prayer can change the one who prays, one's marriage, and one's partner. Don't let a day pass without serious prayer. What can happen will surprise you. Don't be limited to praying only for the ten suggested areas. Here are ten more to get you started:

His past
Her parenting
His sexuality

Her self-image
His attitude
Her words
His example
Her friendships
His contentment
Her priorities

Ultimately, prayer is your best protection. Going through marriage without prayer is like walking a high wire without a safety net. Don't be foolish. Always remember that prayer succeeds when all else fails.

TODAY'S TOOLS

Prayer

Dear God,

Help me to be the best spouse I can possibly be. Forgive me for all the times I have not prayed for my beloved.

When I am angry or frustrated with my spouse, remind me to pray rather than to react. Remind me to pray for my partner every morning, every night, and anytime in between. Bring to my attention all the needs of my beloved. Teach me to pray deeply and sincerely and passionately for him.

If there are other things my partner needs or wishes me to pray for, bring them to my mind.

Thank you for listening to my prayers and taking them seriously. Thank you for being a God who not only hears but also cares enough to answer.

Amen

Passage

Pray at all times and on every occasion in the power of the Holy Spirit.
EPHESIANS 6:18

Practice

① Ask your spouse how you could pray more effectively for his needs. Ask him if he would give you a weekly update of things for which you could pray.
② Find a quiet time and place where you can pray for yourself. Pray for your attitude, your struggles, your bad habits, and anything you do that might possibly hurt your spouse or your marriage.
③ Set aside at least ten minutes each day to pray specifically for your spouse and nothing else. Among other things, be sure to pray for her safety, health, stress, temptations, work, fears, dreams, and faith.

TREASURE YOUR SPOUSE

IN A.D. 1141 WEINBERG CASTLE held more riches than any other single location in all of Europe. If any army could capture this prize, it would be wealthy beyond imagination. Many armies tried, but the men of the castle were fierce and strong and not easily defeated. But one spring the magnificent castle met its match.

A mighty army laid siege of the castle and cut it off from the outside world. The army was patient and its stranglehold deadly. As the months passed, food and water within the castle's walls grew scarce. The defenders gave their rations to the women and children, but starvation could not be held back much longer. Soon death took the gentlest infants and the frailest grandparents. Sorrow touched every family.

The defenders now knew their cause was hopeless, so they agreed to negotiate with their foe. If the women and children were allowed to leave the castle untouched, the men would lay down their weapons and surrender their fortress with its massive storerooms of untold wealth.

The attacking army agreed, but as they moved forward the women of the castle asked for one additional concession. They asked that they each be allowed to take with them as much of their valuables as they could carry. The army pondered the request, and since the treasures of the castle were so great that what the women could carry would be relatively insignificant, they agreed.

What happened next brought emotion to the heart of every soldier who laid siege to the castle. Out of the heavy gates the women came, dressed in their finest gowns. Each woman carried in her arms that thing she treasured most—her husband.

Often it takes a crisis to realize what is of true value. Your spouse is a unique and special person with strengths and talents and potential. Too often, we take that person for granted. Too often we don't treasure a person until after she's gone. Then we finally realize how much she meant to us and how empty life will be without her. Now is the time to treasure your spouse.

Treasure him as your friend. Those couples that are healthiest have learned how to be good friends. Comedian and old-time actor George Burns wrote an entire book, entitled *Gracie: A Love Story*, celebrating his forty-four-year relationship with his wife, Gracie. He described how he treasured her as his loving wife, teammate, and best friend. At the close of his book, he writes, "Marrying Gracie was the best thing that ever happened to me."

We all need friends, and when your spouse is a friend, your marriage doubles in satisfaction. Friendship with your mate chases away your loneliness and turns your home into a safe haven. Friendship also provides an emotional and intellectual connection that deepens your marriage. Emotionally you are embraced and accepted. Intellectually you are respected, though you and your spouse may not always agree. These two connections within a marriage make a secure bond that will protect the marriage from many an outside temptation.

If friendship is so powerful a force within marriage, what exactly is a friend? Friends enjoy spending time together. They accept each other, even when they disagree. Friends know what makes each other smile. They share their hopes, hurts, and deepest secrets without fear of rejection. Friends listen—really listen—with an ear bent on knowing the other person better. They help each other out and are there when things get rough. Friends don't have to have it their way. They resolve conflicts and forgive each other. They are honest and trustworthy, kind and courteous, strong and gentle. Friends stand up for each other.

Treasure her as your encourager. Love believes the best about the other person. What you look for is usually what you find. If you search for beauty and integrity in your spouse, you will find it. If you encourage beauty and integrity, it will grow. The power of encouragement is often underestimated. Encouragement plants acorns and then helps them mature into oaks.

A friend of mine once told me, "I'm a much better person now than I was the day my husband and I got married."

"How did that come to be?" I asked.

"It was my husband," she said with tears in her eyes. "He believed in me when I had lost faith in myself. He loved me when I thought I was unlovable. He encouraged me every day of our marriage. Without him I'd be lost."

Work hard to be your spouse's biggest encourager. Pay attention to her strengths and talents and interests. Be an optimist, and help your spouse believe how special and treasured she truly is. Dry her tears, nurture her potential, applaud her victories, and assist her in turning her dreams into reality. Both husband and wife should be the top cheerleaders of each other. Your job is to encourage and build one other up.

Nowhere in literature is there an encourager greater than Don Quixote. When he looked at Aldonza Lorenza, he saw more than a simple peasant girl. He saw the most beautiful damsel in the world, and he renamed her Dulcinea del Toboso. In his eyes, she was the fairest of the fair. Don Quixote set out to overcome evil and conquer kingdoms, all in the name of his matchless maiden. Even though she insisted that she was no one special, Don Quixote would not waver in his mission. After years of devoted encouragement from Don Quixote, Aldonza finally saw herself through his eyes. As Don Quixote lay dying, she announced she was indeed Dulcinea del Toboso.

Treasure him as your lover. To love and be loved is one of the greatest experiences a person can have. You and your spouse are lovers. This connection should reach out to include every aspect of love, from courtesy to romance to intimacy. Treasure your mate as your beloved, and daily show him the power of unconditional love. Every married person should memorize the definition of unconditional love, found in the love chapter of the Bible:

> *Love is patient and kind. Love is not jealous or boastful*
> *or proud or rude. Love does not demand its own way. Love is*
> *not irritable, and it keeps no record of when it has been wronged.*
> *It is never glad about injustice but rejoices whenever the truth wins out.*
> *Love never gives up, never loses faith, is always hopeful, and endures*
> *through every circumstance. Love will last forever.*
> 1 CORINTHIANS 13:4-8

Francine Rivers's book *Redeeming Love* centers on a character named Sarah who was empty and dead inside. Her mother had passed away when she was a child, and afterwards she had been forced into a life of prostitution. When Michael Hosea saw her, he knew this was not where she belonged. He took her from this lifestyle, married her, and loved her unconditionally.

Yet Sarah was afraid to trust Michael. Two times she ran away, and two times her husband gently, lovingly brought her back home. When Sarah asked him why he kept pursuing someone with her past, he replied, "I love you. You're my wife! . . . I've loved watching you grow and change. . . . I love the way you work. . . . I love watching you skip across the meadow. . . . I love watching you laugh. . . . I love the whole idea of growing old with you and waking up to you every morning for the rest of my life."

Michael knew what being a lover was all about, and Sarah ultimately came to trust him.

Treasure her as your *kokua*. It began with an itch on his right leg. A week later sores appeared on both feet. He grew pale and shivered in the warm weather. By now Mun Ki knew the cause of his misery. He tried all sorts of treatment and medicine, but nothing slowed the spreading of the sores. Finally, he was forced to admit there was no cure for the terrible disease of leprosy.

Three months after the first symptom appeared, Mun Ki sat with his wife and four children eating the evening meal. When the family finished eating, Nyuk Tsin, his wife, sent the children away. She knelt before her husband and said, "I shall be your *kokua*."

This scene, involving a Chinese immigrant couple, happens almost halfway through James Michener's epic novel *Hawaii*. In the late 1800s, people diagnosed with leprosy were immediately banished to a leper colony, called Kalaupapa, on the island of Moloka'i. The government's strategy was "out of sight, out of mind." The officials did allow one provision for comfort—a healthy individual, fully aware of the risks involved, could volunteer to accompany a victim to the leper colony. These people were called *kokuas*, the Hawaiian word for "helpers." A *kokua* lived with and nursed a leper until he died. Then, if the *kokua* had not contracted the disease, he or she was free to return to civilization.

To be a *kokua* took more than love and courage; it took true commitment. Every spouse should be a *kokua*, or helper, to his spouse. Marriage is a total, timeless commitment. It involves giving yourself fully to your spouse, just as Nyuk Tsin did for her husband. Marriage involves sacrifice on your part, but in that sacrifice you find purpose, meaning, and significance. You discover that being a *kokua* and treasuring your spouse as a *kokua* deepens your life and deepens your marriage.

Marriage is a miracle. As you treasure your spouse, he will treasure you. In fact, I've found that when I treasure Tami, I get back two to three times more than what I have given. Treasure your partner in any way you can, but don't forget the couples you've just read about. Treasure your partner as a friend, as an encourager, and as a lover. But most important of all, be his *kokua*.

TODAY'S TOOLS

Prayer

Dear God,

Forgive me for not treasuring my spouse as the most special and valuable gift you have given me.

Remind me that we are friends, and teach me how I might be a true friend in good times and bad.

Remind me that we are encouragers, and open my eyes daily to the many opportunities I have to build up and believe the best about my spouse.

Remind me that we are lovers, and guide me into an unconditional love that bears all things, believes all things, hopes all things, and endures all things.

Remind me that we are kokuas, *and push me beyond my selfishness toward a commitment that is total and timeless.*

Mold me into a spouse who knows how to truly treasure my mate. Give me the strength to treasure my partner beyond what is easy, normal, or humanly possible.

Amen

Passage

Place me like a seal over your heart. . . . Love flashes like fire, the brightest kind of flame. Many waters cannot quench love; neither can rivers drown it. If a man tried to buy love with everything he owned, his offer would be utterly despised. SONG OF SONGS 8:6-7

Practice

① Write a letter, in your own individual style, describing how and why you treasure your spouse. Read to him what you have written, or print it out and give it to him.

② Evaluate what kind of friend, encourager, and lover you have been to your partner in the past month. Determine what you need to do to improve in each of these areas.

③ Go to your spouse—earnestly, humbly, and privately. Kneel before her, take her hand, and commit yourself to be her *kokua* (koh-KOO-uh). Commit yourself to treasure her totally, in any way possible, until the end of your days.

WRAPPING UP

"SHE'S LEFT ME," said a broken voice on the other end of the phone line. "She just left a note on the kitchen table."

"What does it say?" I asked.

"That she doesn't think I love her anymore, and that she can't live in a relationship without love," Gunner sniffed. "We've only been married two years, but she is the light of my life. Without her I'd be lost."

"So why doesn't Kate know you love her?"

"I don't know," he said. "I guess I didn't know how to show her. I did the best I could, but nobody told me what you have to do to be a good husband. My dad left my mom when I was three. After that there were no male role models to teach me what husbands are supposed to know."

"Nobody has ever told you about the rules?" I asked.

"What rules?"

That is the response I usually get when I talk to people about the rules of marriage. Whether we like it or not, life is full of rules. If you want to build a house, you have to follow certain principles. There are rules of engineering, carpentry, and plumbing. You follow the rules and you can have a wonderful house. If you break them, you will have a disaster. Your foundation might be unstable, your pipes might leak, your walls might crack, and ultimately your house might even fall. These rules aren't in place to make things difficult but to make your house strong.

Marriage has its own set of rules. For some, they may be obvious. For others, they may be unexpected. But for everyone, they are surprisingly simple. And these rules don't exist to make your life miserable. Follow these rules and your marriage will grow. It won't be perfect, but it will avoid many of the difficulties that challenge so many other marriages. Break these rules and your marriage will sooner or later be in grave danger.

Gunner listened to the rules. He came to my office and we walked through each one of them until he knew what to do.

"Why didn't anybody tell me about these?" Gunner wondered. "If I had known these things, Kate would still be with me."

Gunner wrote a letter to his wife. He apologized for many things. He explained the rules and how he wanted a second chance to show her how much he truly loved her. He spoke of how he would make her his top priority and how he would treasure her the rest of his life. He asked her to forgive him for his many failures. Then he thanked her for her patience with his selfishness and insensitivity.

Two days later Gunner called me once more.

"Kate was impressed," he said. "She told me that if I was serious about all I wrote, she would give me one more chance. She isn't completely convinced I can do it, Doc, but I'm going to give it the best effort I can muster."

Five years have passed. Gunner and Kate now have two adorable children. If you met them, you'd never guess how close they came to divorce. They look so happy and in love. Kate said recently that her marriage is as perfect as any marriage can be. Then she leaned over and kissed Gunner with a kiss that said more than words.

As the kiss ended, Gunner motioned me to the side. Then with a wink he said, "Thank you for teaching me the rules. They really work."